An Intentional Life

· a guide to a slower and more peaceful existence ·

An Intentional Life

· a guide to a slower and more peaceful existence ·

Kathryn Bardsley of Living The Life You Love

An Intentional Life –
a guide to a slower and more peaceful existence

Copyright © 2021 Kathryn Bardsley
Living The Life You Love

ISBN 978-1-3999-1312-6

www.livingthelifeyoulove.co.uk
@Livinghthelifeyoulove

Credits
Written by Kathryn Bardsley
Quote design by Kathryn Bardsley
Photography by Josey Grace Photography
https://www.joseygrace.com/

Each day that you live life with more intention, is another day well lived.

About The Author

If we haven't met before, Hi! I'm Kay.
I'm a slow and intentional living lifestyle advocate and mindset coach. I inspire and motivate others through my popular life coaching programmes and YouTube channel, Living The Life You Love.

I live in a quaint little English cottage in the Yorkshire countryside with my fiancée and my two adorable cats. I enjoy the simple things in life and I'm a true believer in making more time *to do less.*

I share openly and candidly how I create happy, simple moments for myself each day. My aim is always to inspire others who want something similar for themselves.

The industrialist was horrified to find the fisherman laying beside his boat, smoking a pipe.

- Why arent you fishing?, said the industrialist.

- Because I have caught enough fish for the day.

- Why dont you catch some more?

- What would I do with them?

- Earn more money. Then you could have a motor fixed to your boat and go into deeper waters and catch more fish. That would bring you more money to buy nylon nets, so more fish, more money. Soon you would have enough to buy two new boats, even a fleet of boats. Then you could be rich like me.

- What would I do then?

- Then you could sit back and enjoy life.

- What do you think i'm doing now?

John Lane · Timeless Simplicity

We've all been there at some point.

The day goes by in a blur, one blink and you miss it. You sit wondering how you got to this point, did you make all of the decisions that got you here knowingly?

Have you ever driven or walked to a destination without even thinking twice about which route to take? You get in the car, close the door, turn the key and the next thing you know, you've arrived. At some point your brain switched into a phenomenon I like to call 'autopilot mode'.

This book is about how to switch off autopilot and start to live a more intentional and wholesome life. The kind of life that you're proud of, the kind of life that fills you up, one you can look back on and think fondly about every intentional decision you made as the creator of your own story.

Life isn't about going through the motions to just exist and function on a daily basis, it's about really and truly living in each moment and having a clear vision of who you are. We live in a world filled with hustle and bustle, pulled from pillar to post, living life in the fast lane. It's easy to feel lost and get swept up in the whirlwind that we call life.

The lives we live now are a far cry from the lives our grandparents and great grandparents lived, but the ideals from that time are still faint memories in the distance. We know there is a different way but **how** do you access a calmer life in a world that is built on a 24/7 service with a 'no sleep until you're dead' mentality.

This book is a pause.

It's a gentle reminder to bring more intention into your days so you can enjoy life so much more. It's a reminder of the simple things in life and how easy they are to overlook.

We take a deep dive into all areas of your life to find what is serving you and what isn't. I hope this book acts as a practical guide for you as you walk your own journey. You will find journaling exercises and powerful questions that will help you to find more understanding and clarity.

I hope this book gives you the tools and resources you need to help you to bring more intentionality into your own life. You can either read from start to finish or dip into chapters that resonate to get more of what you love back into your life, and in turn enable you to live a slower, more intentional and much more fulfilled life.

Contents

The foundations of a simple life
What does it mean to live a life with intention?

Ohhh, now there's a question. I felt you flinch a little, I know I did. You start to ponder, your eyes floating off somewhere and your mind starts ticking over… what does it mean, do I do it already? I wish I could do it more…

Sometimes words can put us into boxes, those boxes can feel rigid and downright unforgiving. That's exactly what we don't want to happen here. Instead of only using one word, let's break down the word 'intention' into its key components to make it seem a whole lot less daunting!

I believe there to be 5 parts to being intentional; they all wrap around in a gentle hug and create the ever aspired for "slow life" we all know about but feel is far from our grasp.

Mindfulness
Simplify
Slow down
The bigger picture
Nurture

It's easy to aspire to be someone or to crave something but when you live the kind of life where you're running around like a headless chicken with only one sock on, your phone in the one hand on speakerphone, racing out of the door with a piece of burnt toast in the other, it can feel incredibly far from reach. The truth is, it's not that far away at all. It's just a matter of re-jigging your priorities in life and sitting down and really curating the life you actually want, not the one you seem to have fallen headfirst into.

That's not saying that everyone hates their life, but I'm sure for even the happiest, most fulfilled person on this planet there will be something. It may be small, but something they'd love to have or create in their lives and leading a life filled with intention is the fastest way to get there.

Without intention you have no direction and without direction how do you know where you're going? You're basically living your life with a blindfold on, stumbling around in the dark, bumping into things as you go.

Mindfulness

Mindfulness is a loaded word in today's society which I believe to only be a good thing. With the rise in people meditating and taking time to just chill out a little, mindfulness is never too far away. Be it on the side of a bus, a page in a magazine or an ad on your phone it's there shouting at you to **stop** thinking!

Mindfulness is a funny old word: being mindful is the reason we practice mindfulness... it's kind of an oxymoron in a way. The reason we seek mindfulness is often actually quite the opposite, we desire mind-emptiness. That doesn't have quite the same ring now, does it?

With an empty mind being the goal it's easy to start to feel overwhelmed when you start meditating and your mind is anything but empty... We've all been there, I'm sure. You set yourself a timer and after a few seconds it's like a tidal wave of thoughts. Things that are relevant and things you didn't even know you needed to think about! While meditation is a really important and necessary part of maintaining good mental health, I think there is also an opportunity here to mention that dealing with your full mind and all of its thoughts is also healthy.

When was the last time you truly just let yourself be?

I know for me the most prominent time is when I'm falling asleep at night. You just drift around in a state of contentment, thoroughly entertained by your thoughts (if you're not anxious or in a state of depression, as this can be a totally different experience and one I often deal with myself, but states of mind can change and rest assured, leading an intentional life will only help). This kind of trance-like state is one of bliss; it's your mind focused on only one thing at a time, kind of a miracle in today's crazy world! You are sorting through your to-dos, decompressing from all of the things you did and saw today: conversations, interactions, projects - things not yet complete.

There's a reason why the media often show inspiration striking as someone is trying to get to sleep at night. It's often said we should keep a pen and paper on our bedside table so when it strikes we don't miss it! Imagine giving yourself this opportunity when you're not tired, when you're not the most tired you've been all day… I mean you're in bed, you don't get much more tired than that. Rather, you allow yourself this thinking time when you're wide awake and ready to take on the world, when you could actually do something with it - even if that is just writing it down.

To me, mindfulness isn't just about giving yourself time to be thought free or thought full… It's also about seeing things as they happen. A brilliant example is *a quick shower*. You're probably wondering what I'm on about at this point, but bear with me.

So, when you have a quick shower what do you do? Do you fly into the bathroom, throw your clothes into a heap in the corner, turn the water on and get into it as quickly as you can once it's warm? Sometimes you may be even too impatient to wait for the water to warm up and your feet suffer as you jump into icy cold water. I'm sure you have things you'd like to achieve in the shower, maybe a quick rinse, hair wash or a shave. Once the tick-list is done, out you get. A quick rough dry, throw on some clothes and on you go with your evening. A tight feeling insists in your chest until you finally flop down on the sofa relieved of all your duties for the day.

It's like humanity is in a constant state of rush. It seems everyone is in the process of doing everything at 100 miles an hour. We forget to cherish those simple moments but it's easy to forget that those very moments are what make up our entire life. They fill in all of the spaces like sand between paving stones. Without these moments in between we have no structure and feel a bit wobbly and unsecure.

Let me take you through a more relaxing shower experience.

You open the door and notice the afternoon light streaming into the room. You think to yourself, "what a beautiful afternoon to take a shower, I'm so happy it's sunny today." You take your clothes off and fold them or place them into the laundry bin if they're dirty.

You turn on the shower and as the water is heating you look at yourself in the mirror. You trace the lines on your face with your finger, you smile at yourself and you look deeply into your own eyes. You're in there. Crazy.

The water is hot so you step into the shower feeling warm water on your cold toes, reminding you that after this shower you should really put some socks or slippers on to keep those little piggies warm. They truly deserve it after keeping you standing all day. You feel the water running over your skin, you have goosebumps where the water isn't hitting as the air around you is cold. You rub your arms feeling the bumps on your skin start to retreat as your skin warms. There is a delightful choice of shower gels to choose from, one for each mood you could be in.

You're feeling really happy and content so you are torn between the choice of two scents, orange or rose. You smell both and in the end you go with rose as it feels the most comforting and orange might be too stimulating towards the end of the day. Aren't bubbles the most joyful thing?

You swish them all over your body and thoroughly enjoy the peaceful scent before you wash them off and see them flowing down your legs and making a whirlpool as they escape down the drain. You turn the water off and hear the handle let out a little squeak that sounds so familiar, only your shower does that. Suddenly you feel so cosy and warm knowing you're home and in your happy place.

You take the time to dry yourself with your warm towel that you thoughtfully put on the radiator to warm before stepping into the shower. Then you reach down to pick up the pajamas that you chose to wear for tonight. Soft. You chose your softest most luxurious feeling pjs, only the best after a long day.

 You feel a sense of calm wash over you as you leave the bathroom. You left the day behind in there, you intentionally let it wash down the drain and it feels *so good.*

Another example that I'm sure is a part of most people's morning routines is a nice hot cup of tea or coffee. Oh how easy it is to drink your coffee down in one big gulp feeling frantic and stressed that you're running out of time to drink it!

It's too easy to hit snooze one last time when you're in bed in the morning, you open your eyes and feel that all too familiar stinging feeling and wave of dread washing over you, knowing that it's nearly time to face the day. You may think "oh well, I'll just have to rush a little more but I'm so tired and sleep is more important than anything else". But the truth is, you're not gaining any more time in your day by sleeping in.

Those extra twenty minutes of broken sleep aren't contributing anything to your day, all they are doing is putting you on a hamster wheel from the moment you open your eyes.

I honestly believe one of the worst feelings you can let yourself experience is the feeling of not being able to drag yourself out of bed when your alarm goes off in the morning. Usually this is caused by not having enough restful sleep that night or not drinking enough water the day before. This groggy state of being upon rising is a state most people exist in until the afternoon.

Not only does it feel awful being tired it also means you've instantly broken a promise to yourself and doing that every single day is a sure-fire way to wear away at your own self discipline and self confidence.

Now let's compare two mornings and see what can happen if you give yourself time to enjoy life, rather than rush through it.

Snoozing the morning away

"Uuuuughhh, it can't be time to get up already. Five more minutes" Last night's Netflix marathon is finally catching up with you. Unfortunately, those extra five minutes turn into an extra twenty minutes and this puts you massively behind for the rest of your morning routine. You have to start cutting things out. Shower? Never mind. Oats for breakfast? No time. Plain toast will have to do. You pace around the kitchen as you wait a torturous few minutes for the toast to pop up, you're sure time is going backwards.

You pour your instant coffee into a flask not waiting for it to cool first and off you go out of the front door. You pile your things into the boot of the car carelessly, you haven't time for patience or care this morning. You're in a bad mood because you feel so stressed and resentful that you don't have time to do anything other than work. As you sit in the car confronted with rush hour traffic that is making you even more late, you take a sip of your much needed coffee. "Ah! TOO HOT". You say to yourself "Tomorrow will be better, I can't keep doing this" but guess what? Unless you break the cycle of going to bed late or ignoring your alarm the cycle will never end.

Up bright and early

Your alarm goes off and you roll over to turn it off. You're feeling a little tired this morning but you're also feeling relaxed and content. The house is warm from the central heating that was set to come on for you waking. You put on your snuggliest soft dressing gown and go and indulge in a lovely hot shower, the best way to start the day.

Downstairs you pop the coffee machine on and froth some milk, one of your favourite rituals of the day. Sweet soothing nectar soon to warm your stomach. Your porridge oats ping in the microwave and you cut yourself some sweet, juicy fresh fruit to go on top. You put it on in a way that looks so pleasing and pretty and you find yourself smiling in admiration or your pretty porridge.

You sit on the sofa and take your first sip of coffee. You take a moment to appreciate the delightful smell of freshly brewed coffee before feeling it warming your hands. You sit for a few minutes pondering the day, the tasks you have ahead of you and feel grateful for this moment you've carved out for yourself.

Everything happens just as it should, you leave right on time and manage to miss the rush hour traffic. You're in a good mood and that reflects on your entire day. You may have been a little tired this morning but your reward for getting up and starting your day slowly has already outweighed the tiredness you felt.

Can you see the difference between these routines? Some people like to believe they thrive on chaos but living in a high stress environment and leading a chaotic lifestyle is bound to cause burn out at some point in your life. Feeling constantly stressed and anxious leads to you putting your body in a fight or flight response.

This causes high cortisol and adrenaline levels in your body, hormones that are helpful if we need to protect ourselves or be extremely alert but not helpful to lead a calm or relaxed life. Usually, these levels return back to normal once the stressful experience is over but if you're putting yourself under too much pressure and causing yourself to feel anxious a lot of the time they will stay elevated. Long term overexposure to these stress hormones can cause a whole host of health conditions such as: IBS, Muscle Tension, Headaches and Heart Disease.[1]

We all have stressful days or periods of our lives which are unavoidable but analysing your current life, patterns and routines to find areas where you're causing excess pressure and stress will help you to find more calm in your daily life.

Simplify

It's easy to overthink simplicity, especially when trying to create a more intentional life. By doing this you're unintentionally overcomplicating the simplest of things! This in turn puts more pressure on yourself and causes you to be more overwhelmed in the long run.

Instead, just think about what you do or experience in your everyday life that could be made more simple. Here are a few questions to help to spark something inside of you -

· What is something that makes you feel stressed on a daily basis?

· Does your home environment bring you joy?
  - What could you change to make you feel more content?
  - When you think about your perfect afternoon at home, what comes to mind?

- Is there something you do that could make your days easier?
    - What would a peaceful but achievable morning/evening routine for you look like?

- Do you plan meals for the week ahead?
    - Can you bulk make meals to have access to healthier food in a busy week?
    - What recipes can you make that call for similar ingredients, or ingredients that you already have in the cupboard?

- What is your beauty/self care routine like?
    - Does it have lots of steps, does that make it unachievable on a daily basis?
    - Can you pick your favourite parts and try to include a less complex version on a daily basis?

- Does gift giving cause you stress?
    - Can you have an honest conversation with your loved ones and try to find out what they would really like? (I'm sure the answer would be to cause you less stress!)
    - I truly believe experiences are the best gifts to give, as is your time. Instead of expensive presents, try giving your loved ones an experience. That might be afternoon tea for two or a day of exploring a city, maybe a trip to the theatre or for little ones an afternoon at a play area followed by their favourite restaurant/meal.

Not only are you giving them a 'gift' you're also giving to yourself: you get to enjoy the experience with them and also watch them enjoying themselves – everyone wins.

Simplicity really is key in my own personal experience. I spent years with complicated beauty & self-care routines and buying things to make my home feel 'perfect' but in the end it just caused me to feel more stress, have less time and less money. When it comes to your home, think about your cleaning routine. Do you have one? What products do you use? How could you simplify it?

As consumers, we're led to believe we need a different product for every single item in our home, but the truth is you really don't. If you're on a tight budget, do yourself a favour and buy some distilled vinegar, a big bulk bag of baking soda and a few lemons. Find an old spray bottle and you've just got yourself the cheapest cleaning ingredients to keep your home and your purse in good shape. I like to buy multipurpose cleaning sprays, that way I can use them all around my home for lots of different items and I don't need five other bottles that probably have exactly the same results!

There is no shame in buying products if that is what serves you but I know in my experience opening up my cupboard and seeing it overflowing with bottles makes me want to close it right back up again. Instead imagine opening it and seeing a nice organised space. A few bottles of cleaning products in order of what you use most and a few cleaning cloths.

Simple. Easy. Achievable. This mantra goes into all areas of life too.

You can use the same principle and apply it to anywhere in your home or any area of your life. Have a think about the current state of your wardrobe, your bathroom cabinet, your bedroom drawers, your store cupboards.

When you open them up, what do you currently see? What would you rather see? How would that make you feel?

Write yourself a little list of areas of your home you could simplify and how you will achieve these changes.

Area 1:
What I will change -

-
-
-
-

Area 2:
What I will change -

-
-
-
-

Area 3:
What I will change -

-
-
-
-

Area 4:
What I will change -

-
-
-
-

Slow down

It's time to start living in the slow lane. When we slow down, we make more space for all that we love. We give ourselves time to actually breathe and to assess what we want to do with our precious time, which over time turns into our precious life.

It's easy to take life for granted sometimes. We get so busy making plans that we forget to live, but life really is all about living and if all you do is go through the motions to get through a day, your life will go by in a *big blurry haze*. One day you may well look back and wonder where all that time went and wish for more days.

Well, those days are now and I'm here to *give them back to you.*

No Plans Days

I know it sounds counterintuitive to what I just said, but making no plans opens your days up to so much more. If you have structure and routine every single day of your life you have no room for spontaneity, and spontaneity is where the true magic happens.

If I were to give you an extra hour in your day today, what would you do with it?

Sometimes we get so stuck in our patterns and routines that we don't leave enough space for the things that make us truly happy. That is what makes No Plans Days so special, you don't only have one hour extra, you have given yourself an entire day to enjoy moment by moment without any pressure or expectation.

Sit with yourself and see what comes up for you with the idea of making zero plans this weekend. What does it stir up inside of you? Stress, worry, the feeling of it not being 'enough'? Or maybe you feel relieved or excited about the idea. The thing with this is that it's an oxymoron - although it's a no plan day, you are also planning to have no plans that day. Ironic, I know.

The thing is, if someone says to you, "What are you doing at the weekend? I thought you could come over or we could go to … and then do … and have you seen … in a while? I know they'd like to see you, maybe you should go see them this weekend."

I'm sure we've all had experiences with people like this, maybe even loved ones who are a huge part of your life but you're well within your rights to say, "No I'm having a no plans day, but we could do that another day"

Own it.

Don't let other people dictate what you do with your time.

If you've spent your entire life doing what other people want you to do it's going to take some time to put in boundaries and for those people to accept that they truly **don't** own **your** time. Maybe this person doesn't exist in your life, maybe you are this person. Either way, give yourself space to breathe and to step back for at least one day of the month.

I felt the urge here to list what you could do on a no plans day but that would totally defeat the purpose as the whole point is not to plan it, but to see what happens. You know yourself what you would do if you were given the time and freedom. Release the guilt attached and just let yourself think about what you would do. Free time doesn't always have to be productive. The phrase "when I have time to waste" came up recently with one of my life coaching clients and I caught her in her tracks. It isn't about wasting the time you have or even filling it with anything at all. It's about *enjoying* your time. It's about doing what feels right for you in that exact moment. That might mean you want nothing more than to put your feet up and catch up on the latest series you've been watching. It could also mean you really want some child free time. Time to have no responsibility for a while. Maybe you have a project you really want to work on but feel guilty when you do. It might have been a long time since you had time to go for a walk by yourself and gather your thoughts. This is the time you're creating for the things you love. You're not wasting your time by having a zero plans day, you're giving yourself the opportunity to enjoy your free time *more.*

When was the last time you enjoyed a coffee in bed? A walk in the garden? Read a book to your child, or a book to yourself? Spent time cleaning your home? Had a good old clear out? Sit with this for a while and then factor a 'no plans' day into this month and see what magic comes of it.

Travel

I've spent a lot of the last 5 years of my life travelling all around the world which I was very privileged to be able to afford to do and I feel extremely grateful for but in turn, I also have some great wisdom to share with you from harsh lessons I learnt along my journey.

I had a wonderful time gallivanting around with not a care in the world. I ticked so many things off my bucket list and did so many things that I'd never even considered doing before, like swimming with seals! If you ever have the opportunity, definitely do it. I've never felt as free as I did playing and swimming with wild seals in the open ocean. It was a magical experience that I will never forget. The problem was I did so much all the time that I got in the routine of doing that much.

If I wasn't doing *something,* I felt I was wasting my precious time and money being on the other side of the world. Every day gone was a day I would never get back and I was another day closer to going home.

I experienced *burnout*. Burnout like I've never felt before. The stress of having to plan every single thing, factor in a budget and fleeting money, not having enough days to do everything I wanted to do in a place…the constant feeling of time running out. I experienced burn out so bad that one sunny day I found myself in Hawaii in a hostel room under my covers crying because I felt so overwhelmed and depressed.

Hawaii was always my 'dream'. If you'd have asked me in the past where my dream holiday or place to live was, I would always say HAWAII!! I'd idolised it for so long that when I finally got there, I felt my life grind to a dramatic, ear-screeching halt. All I could think was how can I be in (in my opinion) the most beautiful place in the world and feel so, so, so miserable?

The truth is that up until arriving there I'd felt I was on a hamster wheel running from one place to the next. Tick, tick, tick. Done, what's next? Where next? What is there to do there? What does the calendar look like? Do we have time? How much money do we have left?

I was enjoying myself and the experiences I was having but my travels were coming to an end much faster than I would have liked... Reality was catching up with me and I was nowhere near ready to leave traveling behind me. I was due home in just a month after being away for nearly a year and a half. I appreciate how privileged this experience must seem and to some it would be a really great problem to have but the problem was - I was running from myself.

I felt like everything I needed to be happy was in the next place or the next experience.

Hawaii grounded me and healed me in lots of ways. I sat with that dark cloud and over time it started to lift.

I remembered that *I am home.*

Wherever you go, there you are.

Seek comfort in discomfort. There's always something to learn, you just have to look for the lesson and be willing to listen and accept.

You take you with you wherever you go. If you don't look after yourself you can't expect an external source to bring you happiness. You have to find peace in yourself first.

When planning holidays and little trips away, ask yourself first what is it that is going to serve you? I'm not saying that when you go away you should do absolutely nothing, rather, you should do what you want to do. Not what you feel like you **should** do.

Maybe what you're really craving is nothing but sunshine, cocktails and sleep! On the contrary you might be after time spent in the mountains and days filled with adventures. Make sure your plans align with what your soul needs and you can't go too far wrong.

The bigger picture

A lot of what I'm speaking about in this book is to get you to step out of your logical mind and to start to hone in and to tap into your own intuition. Some people find it easy to trust their inner voice while others really struggle and shut it down constantly with facts and figures. The problem with this is if you never make space for the unknown you will never have the opportunity to feel the gratification that comes when you trust that little voice inside and good comes from it. The more you listen to that voice the easier it is to hear and the more your life and the daily choices you make will be made from the heart rather than the mind.

Life is constantly conflicting itself. There is no such thing as 'balance', it's a word that just doesn't fit into a human life, as much as we'd like it to. Humanity has led itself to believe humans are perfection and we can do no wrong but the reality is we are not robots. Society likes to think we are but we are far from it. We constantly make mistakes and those mistakes are what make us human. Without mistakes some of the greatest creations in the world would never have been made. There has to be room for error.

Black and white aren't the only options we have, instead a lot of life is spent in various shades of grey. Some of us are great at routine and structure, some may feel suffocated by the very thought. We're all different and need different things at different times in our lives.

The pendulum is constantly moving because *so are you.*

You're an animate being with thoughts, feelings, emotions and desires and they are always shifting and changing. Life never stops changing and the realisation that nothing is ever staying the same is a powerful, life changing one. It can stir up big emotions in people.

I remember the first time I realised that my current life would not always be as it was. I think I was about 12 years old. I realised that one day I would be older; I would have a job, maybe even children of my own; that I would be a grandparent one day and I would have people in my life in that moment in time that I have never met. Those people I was thinking about didn't currently exist and strangely haven't ever been thought about until the very moment I sat realising this. My mind was blown. I just couldn't understand how everything I knew would just change. It all felt so raw. So unapologetic. I wasn't ready to accept that fact at that very moment.

The thing is, as I've got older, I've come to realise that there is beauty in change. There is a growth more powerful than I've ever experienced. Change is also a form of growth. Growth can take many forms, emotional, physical or even sometimes both at the same time. Changes, no matter how small, can be quite challenging. It's in difficult times that we truly find who we are. Our morals, values and opinions are challenged and we're forced to re-assess.

To me that is what life is all about. It's about making sure you're living in alignment with who you truly are and that can only happen with change, big or small. The beauty is in knowing that every decision you make you affirm even more who you are and what you stand for. You can look back and see how you've flourished over the years and how that never would have happened if nothing ever changed in your life.

One of the hardest things about change is grieving what once was. Grieving is an important process for our minds, it helps us to process what has happened and allows us to find ways to deal with the pain we feel. The main problem can arise if you never stop grieving the past. When this happens, you go into a state of resistance: you won't embrace change or allow yourself to move forward. But change is a good thing. Good things come from it, trust me.

Living in the past doesn't help to move you forward but it also doesn't move you back towards what you're grieving for. The past is in the past. You just get stuck.

But life keeps moving and *so do you.*

Imagine being on an escalator. It keeps moving you closer and closer to the top and when you get there you say, "No way am I ready to get off!" and so you resist. It keeps pushing you and you keep having to push back so you don't fall down. People keep coming and shoving you out of the way and the whole thing makes you feel miserable.

At some point you have to accept that life is going to keep putting obstacles in your way and rather than putting up a shield to deflect them you have to walk with them. As you would on an escalator, there comes a point in time when the easy ride is over and you have to make a decision to step forward and start walking again by yourself. You have to get back to reality.

At some point you have to start moving your feet forward again and embrace the fact that **change always is.**

While I feel 'no plans days' are important, what is also important is your bigger life picture.

What are you here for?
What do you feel called to do?
What fills your cup?

Woah, I know. Loaded questions. I remember about six years ago sitting on my childhood bed watching Ted Talk after Ted Talk about 'my life purpose' or 'how to find your life mission' and just feeling completely lost. I had no idea what I wanted to do with my life and do you know what? Six years later, I still don't!

What changed is I now know what I love. I know what serves me and what makes me feel happy and content. If you never stop to think about how you feel in your life it becomes very easy to go into robot mode, or as I called it earlier on 'autopilot mode'.

To help you find your deeper purpose I have created an exercise. Do this in your own time and be sure to set the mood so you feel comforted and at ease. It's a really heavy topic and can be quite triggering for some people. Maybe your life is all sorted and the idea of uprooting it and starting again makes you want to scream! The fact it can bring such strong emotions means it's important and honouring your desires is the fastest way to a happier and more content life.

Finding your purpose is honestly a lifetime of work. Some people never truly figure it out; others figure it out without even realising. The thing is your purpose in life is fully able to change its path, just as you are able to change and grow. What once served you no longer does and your purpose in life should be no different.

The perfect day

Imagine you've just woken up from a deep restful sleep. You open your eyes and you're in a dream world. It's a perfect day. Nothing can go wrong today. Where are you? What does the world feel like, smell like, look like? What are your plans for the day? What do you do first? How do you feel? What are you wearing? Play through your day from waking up to going to bed that night, feeling and thinking like you're really experiencing everything that happens.

Close your eyes and think deeply about this. There is no right or wrong. Don't let limiting self belief get in the way of this exercise.

Dream your wildest dreams even if they seem far from reach.

What does your perfect day look like?

_____

_____

_____

_____

_____

_____

_____

_____

_____

_____

_____

_____

Now read back what you've written, how far is this vision from your current reality? Is there anything you can take from this vision and implement into your current life and daily routines? If not, what steps can you take to get yourself to a place where you're able to?

Sometimes it's easy to overlook what we already have in our lives but the person who you are today and how you live your life is what is going to show up tomorrow and the next day. Changing your daily rhythms and routines to match where you want to go is a fast way to get you to your vision much quicker.

Rocking Chair Vision

If you're feeling stuck and unsure about what your purpose is or what you want to contribute to the world, try getting out of your current state of mind and into a completely different one.

Take a moment to imagine yourself as 90 years old. You're sitting in your cosy living room in your comfy rocking chair, slowly rocking back and forth pondering your life and all you've achieved. This is you having lived your dream life where all possibilities came true. This is an opportunity to explore what happens when they really do.

What words describe who you are as a person?
What values do you hold?
What brings you a sense of happiness and fulfilment?

What do you do for fun and leisure?
What are you proud of?
What have you learned?
Where are you?
How do you feel?
Why do you feel that way?

_____

_____

_____

_____

_____

_____

_____

_____

_____

_____

_____

Reading back what you've just written you should now feel more clear and certain about what it is that you **do** and **don't** want for your life. With that kind of clarity it is easier to move forward and to work towards the life of your dreams. How you feel about what you have written may well change over time, so don't be afraid to revisit this exercise in the future.

As I said before, I still have no idea what my true life purpose is but each day that I focus on what I love I'm getting closer and closer to finding it. Try not to put too much pressure on yourself as that can feel completely overwhelming. I think it's horrendous that in the UK in Year 9 when you're 13/14 years old, you're asked to choose what subjects you want to study for the next two years of your life. These subjects are the basis or what you want to do with the rest of your life, they can influence what college courses you can get onto and then what university degree and jobs you can do. Imagine being 13 years old, not a care in the world and BOOM...

What career do you want to do for the rest of your life?

Most have no clue. I know I didn't. Growing up I was asked all the time. My answer would change constantly. Hairdresser, vet, teacher, nurse, astronaut, photographer, midwife. Why do we put so much pressure on such young children?

Maybe because we don't know ourselves.

I now never ask a child what they want to be when they grow up, I know the pressure that brings. I just let them enjoy their childhood. Rather than asking this, ask what is their favourite way to spend their free time, where they want to go on holiday, what their dream pet would be... Fun, silly questions for children whose brains aren't even fully developed yet.

I was always interested in art as a child. If it was the only lesson I could ever do, I would in a heartbeat. I spent all of my free time painting, drawing, and creating. It felt only natural to take art as a subject when I chose my options at school. The problem for me occurred two years later. It was no longer a hobby, it was an obligation. It was endless coursework, deadlines, homework, forced creativity. It killed my passion. After I left school I didn't pick up a pencil to draw for about five years. I still haven't fully got back the passion for art I once had but I have found new ways to use the creativity I was born with.

I found new ways to honor that little creative spark inside of me. I started editing videos for YouTube and filming myself living my daily life, putting lots of thought into the shots and what feeling I wanted to portray. With this I've found that I get such a brilliant creative release.

Did I know at 14 that I wanted to create and edit videos for a living? No! I had no idea that was even an option but I've found this path by following my intuition and my passions.

What they don't tell you when you're in school is that nobody truly knows what they want to do because their interests are constantly changing. There is no shame in changing your mind. You're allowed to change career paths at 16, 20, 50, even 70! Nobody can tell you how to live your life and there is nothing ever stopping you from reaching higher. Do the course, take the test, do the interview. Apply for a job you think you will never get in a million years. What is stopping you? Self doubt. Don't let it get in your way.

Find what brings you joy and **do more of it.**

I love sharing, I love helping people to feel happy and content. I like helping others to make big shifts in their lives and seeing them reap the benefits. I like being cosy, I like inspiring others to do the same. I've set up my life so that I can share intentional living and while it helps and inspires you, it also feeds my soul. I like to believe my work really makes an impact on other people's lives and that in turn makes me very happy.

Win, win!

Curate your days so that you can do things that build you up and feed that little spark inside of you. After completing the exercises above, you should have a better understanding of what you're craving more of in your life which will help you to create more structure to ensure you make time for it.

Nurture

If you don't look after your body, where will you live?

It's easy to go about your day forgetting that your body exists. I imagine we've all had those weird moments where you suddenly remember you have a body and that you're alive. Nurturing yourself is the most important thing you'll ever do. There are so many ways you can nurture yourself and it's down to you to figure out what fills up your life cup. Have a think about what you love to do if nobody is around, or what makes you excited to speak about or to do. If you're an artist maybe it's creating art with no boundaries or expectations – a writer may just love to keep a journal and for nobody else to ever read the words!

These small things really add up and I like to think of them as little acts of kindness to ourselves. Self-love is something that society really needs to value more and the more you practice self-love the better at nurturing yourself you become.

These little acts of kindness really don't need to stop there either! Let it overflow into all areas of your life. To people you love, your home, your pets, your garden, your treasured items. Spend time creating *real* connections and practise flowing throughout your days with a kind heart thinking kind thoughts. We all have bad days where our mind is dark and our thoughts negative but next time you have a negative thought, try to think of a positive one too.

People often ask how I am such a positive person and this really is just how. I rewired my thinking! I still have anxious and negative thought loops but I also always look for a bright side. Life is a lot more cheery when everything isn't doom and gloom, trust me.

When it rains
look for rainbows
when it's dark
look for
stars

Wisdom from our elders
What we can learn from those who
walked this path before us

It's easy to forget that the way things are now isn't the way things have always been. Humanity has changed a lot even just in the last 50 years. I remember when I was younger, I was given a homework assignment to ask my grandparents about the second world war. My mind was blown that they were alive at that time. A time when black and white pictures were a thing and TV's didn't exist! I still remember being in awe and lusting after that era, I still think of that era as 'the glory days' though it was definitely a much more challenging time to exist.

My grandparents would have only been very young but old enough to remember and most certainly old enough to remember the stories their parents and grandparents had told them. I was fascinated hearing my Grandad recount what it was like to hide in a bunker and hearing the sirens and my Nannan's tales of having to use ration cards and bathing in a tin bath in front of the fire in a house with no central heating.

She had to wait for the water to get warm from the fire before she could get in and everyone in the house used the same water. By the time everyone was washed the water could be so murky you couldn't see through it. That's where the phrase "don't throw the baby out with the bath water" comes from, eldest first – youngest last. I love this phrase. If you ever hear someone say it, it basically means don't make an avoidable error when trying to get rid of something bad by accidentally also getting rid of something good!

It's like another world and it is, in fact, a lifetime ago. Ask your grandparents, parents or other elders in your life about what they remember. It's a really wonderful thing to do, to ask about the past. Hear their stories and let those stories live on through you when the younger generation in turn ask you.

We can learn **a lot** from the old ways. When was the last time you were truly hungry? Went without a bath or shower? Felt cold and had no way of warming up other than putting more clothes on? Actually used a monthly budget when shopping? Appreciated how amazing it is to have a home and space to exist? I know this isn't the reality for every person in the world and a lot of people and societies do really struggle but I'm speaking here, to you. The person reading this book who had enough disposable income to invest in themself...

But what can we learn?

There has never been a society so hell-bent on hurry and 'the grind'. We live in a society that favours busy and cheers on those in a rush with no time to spare!

There are so many books out there about how to succeed and do better and fit more in and do this, do that. But where are the books about the opposite? Is there any value in doing less? Does society see this as a waste of time? If you do less, are you not contributing? Is your happiness and peace of mind worth absolutely nothing?

I don't believe so. I believe it's more important than *anything* else. Without happy healthy humans society doesn't work. There is only so far we can go before we burn out. You see it time and time again in films, tv programs, in books and even just when speaking to friends and family. We are not robots. We need time to be human, we need time to just **be**.

We can learn to **tune out.**

A poor life this if,
full of care.
We have no time to stand
and stare

W.H. Davies

If your current reality is far too fast paced, think of ways you can slow down and take a slower pace in life. Simple little swaps, like instead of watching TV after you eat your evening meal, prioritise cooking from scratch. Take a little longer to actually nourish yourself rather than that quick and easy ready meal or frozen pizza with no nutrition and lots of unhealthy preservatives. Sit with your family and catch up with their days, tell stories, ring a loved one or play board games. Connect. Connection is something that is being lost these days and without connection it is easy to lose purpose in life.

Convenience is just that. Convenient. There's a reason this is seen as one of the best times to be alive. We have everything we ever need right at our fingertips, just at the click of a button. Times have changed and now we're moving faster than ever before. I'm still amazed that in some parts of the country you can order something on Amazon and it arrives the same day.

Gone are the days where you had to wait weeks for something to arrive. While it's great and 'convenient' it also takes away the shine. It takes away the wait and the pining. It takes pressure off the decision to buy it and makes it easier to throw it away.

Imagine you pay £5 for a t-shirt. It arrives, you try it on and you realise it doesn't fit quite right or it wasn't what you expected. How easy would it be to throw it into the back of your wardrobe and tell yourself you'll deal with it later? I know I've been guilty of this in the past. Later comes and it's decluttering time! You empty your wardrobe and guess what's still there? The £5 t-shirt with the tag still on, never worn. You throw it into the donation pile and feel great about how much you're decluttering! But is it great? Is that not really wasteful? That t-shirt could have never been bought in the first place or could have been returned and sent to a new home. You could have bought a better quality tshirt that when you donate will last the recipient years to come.

If the t-shirt cost £50 you'd be far less inclined to throw it to the back of the cupboard and forget about it. You'd deal with it right away - no way are you going to throw £50 away just like that! How wasteful and disrespectful of the time it took you to earn that money.

If you do or have ever forgotten to return an expensive item that you bought and don't want/need, think about that for a moment. Why don't you respect the time it takes you to work and earn money? Why do you buy things you don't need/want and then in turn waste your money and more importantly your time?

As I said before, all of this 'time' makes up your life. You're literally wasting your life every time you do this.

Everything you do in life is an energy exchange. That crumpled up £50 t-shirt in the bottom of your wardrobe is a direct reflection of how you're living your life right now. Harsh I know, but also true.

This is where a change of mindset comes in. People tend to value time/worth more when spending large amounts of money. That money needs to be well spent, you worked hard for it. You might feel resistant to the idea of buying a t-shirt for £50 and even scoff at the thought! But you might happily buy 5 really low quality t-shirts from a fast fashion brand with terrible ethical practices that you know won't fit right after their first wash.

When I'm buying anything new I think of 'cost per wear/use'. How many times would I need to wear or use an item before I feel I've got my money's worth? A great example of this is a coffee machine.

We recently bought ourselves a fancy new coffee machine. We very rarely go out for a coffee but when we do we always enjoy it so much more than the instant coffee we make at home.

For us the good experience doesn't come from going to the coffee shop, rather it comes from the coffee itself. There's nothing better than a good cup of coffee. I realised this and thought, "Why don't we just get a nice coffee machine?." Can I afford it? I sat with the idea for a month or two and then decided to go for it.

It was a large investment but now we save money from having to go out to buy coffee and instead can enjoy a well made latte at home! We use the machine multiple times a day and if you ask me, it paid itself off within the first week.

What is important to note here is that sometimes higher ticket items are too far out of reach and there's no shame in buying something cheaper, of lesser quality, to fill the gap until you can afford to upgrade or replace it.

Being intentional with when you buy is just as, if not **more** important than what you buy. You should never sell yourself short just so you can buy a new item.

Convenience always has a price to pay. Be it time, cost or impact.

For example:

Convenience and reason why	Impact/ downside	Solution	Outcome/ New Impact
Store bought tea bags easy & convenient	Plastic in the ocean May be sprayed with pesticides Negatively impacts society where it's grown	Use loose leaf tea and a reusable tea strainer Grow my own tea herbs in my garden	Less plastic consumption Better for environment I feel good about it New hobby growing herbs
Buying from cheap clothing stores Convenient & affordable	Negative impact on environment & society Overconsumption on Lessens meaning when clothes are so cheap	Only buy from these retailers when really necessary Try to buy better natural materials over synthetics Look in charity/thrift stores first	I feel good about what I wear & I'm aware of it's impact I only buy what I need I value what I own

The important thing here is that you start to slowly work towards these new solutions. You don't have to take on the entire world in a day but being honest with yourself and calling yourself out on these things is a good way to start. Question your actions right now and ask yourself if you're living in line with your morals and values.

A quick note on this – I myself have struggled with my physical and mental health in the last few years. I would once pride myself on being as zero waste as I could be but poor health can change how we view the world. Things can become overwhelming and the weight of the world on your shoulders makes decisions harder to make so in turn you default back to what is familiar. I'm working back towards being the best version of myself and if you relate to this please don't be too hard on yourself.

There are many areas of life where one size doesn't fit all. Maybe you have a disability and buying vegetables ready sliced in a plastic bag makes your life so much easier and makes healthy food accessible. Maybe you need a straw to drink. Maybe you don't have a car and the only shop you have close by doesn't have many options. Or maybe money doesn't quite stretch that far at the end of a month. Only you know your true 'truth' and your opinion should be the only one that matters to you.

What areas of your life do you prioritise convenience and what impact do these decisions have?

Convenience and reason why	Impact/ downside	Solution	Outcome/ New Impact

The next time you want to buy something, put it on a waiting list. Write yourself a little note of what it is you want, how much it costs and why you want it. I know it sounds like quite a lot of hassle but if you're a shopaholic this can really stop you in your tracks. Have you ever tried a 30 day no spend challenge? I can tell you first hand it is NOT easy but do you know what? It is a really interesting way to look deeper into your own psyche.

You can start to see patterns of spending and times when you feel the need to buy instead of dealing with your emotions. For me my worst time of month for spending is the week leading up to my period. I like to call it my 'nesting phase'. I see this as me getting my home and environment all nice and cosy ready to have a calm and more comfortable period. But do I need new 'stuff' to have a nicer period? No. Will I be just fine without it? Yes!

If I find myself feeling like I want a new pair of pajamas or something cute for the house I write it on a list and see if I still want it next month. If I start to feel panicked by it, like I need it NOW, I know even more that I don't. I'm buying to fill a void and so I resist. The more you resist these things the easier it will become.

Be aware, sometimes this can bring up lots of emotion especially if like me you tend to get spendy just before your period. Hormone levels are high as are emotions but it's worth it in the end.

Another weak spot for me has been the supermarket. I try to limit myself to going once a week when I can. If I go more times than this, I can end up spending way more money than I want to on unnecessary items that could have just waited until next week. Before I know it I'm drifting off into the homeware section and that's that!

Goodbye hard-earned money. Hello new mug.

It might not seem so bad. An extra £5 on a shopping bill this week and an extra £10 next week but it all starts to add up over time. When I was at a really low point in my life, I would dread even logging onto my bank account. Embarrassed and ashamed to see where that month's wage had disappeared to. Then one day I forced myself to add up all of the unnecessary expenses I had made that month and was horrified with the number that stared back at me on the calculator screen. In that very moment something within me changed. I realised that I needed to stop splurging and I needed to respect myself and my time more

There's nothing wrong with getting nice new things from time to time but if every time you go into a store you look for something new to buy that you don't need, start to ask yourself, why? Why do you do that? Is it a habit? Do you find enjoyment from it? Are you hoping to find something?

I've had times when I know I can't spend any more money that month and I still go down the aisle 'to window shop' but I feel suffocated the entire time! What if there is something I like? How do I justify it? What if it's not there next week? Instead of torturing yourself, find some discipline and walk straight out of the aisle.

Go to the check out and leave.
You can't shop in a headspace like that.

That goes for any form of shopping at all, in person or online. If you're in a bad headspace you may find yourself acting from a place of lack or need. Neither of these make you feel good in the long run. When you leave the store with no new unnecessary items take pride in that. Take a moment to thank yourself and to realise that decision came from a place of self love rather than self sabotage.

What have you bought this month that you didn't really need? Let's get raw here. Log onto your bank account and be vulnerable for a moment. There is only you who will see this list.

Don't include food shopping and items that sustain you but do include anything you see as excessive. This changes for each person but for me that would be store bought coffee, eating out for convenience rather than pleasure. Buying items I don't need or could have waited to get for a special occasion.

Date purchased	Item	Cost
	Total =	

Are you horrified? Are you proud? Can you notice any patterns here? Are there certain times of the month that you find you spend more? Is there any way you could hold yourself accountable by banning yourself from spending at this time? Is there an accountability partner you could run potential purchases past to see if they feel you need it, or get their opinion on whether the item is worth the cost?

Now let's create a new list that you can keep coming back to. Let's make a 'wait list' and put everything onto this list that you currently feel the urge to bring into your life.

Think of every single little thing. It might not seem necessary but it really helps you to not impulse buy and instead helps you find the nicest version of what you want for the best value. For example, you might need a new notebook. You could just get one from the supermarket but then what if you see one in a bookstore that is so much prettier? You'll buy that too and suddenly you have two notebooks when you only needed one.

So instead of making that notebook an impulse buy, really think about what you want the item to look like, what function it will have and how it will make you feel before you bring it into your life. This is one of the biggest ways I've turned my shopping habits around and also made my purchases more intentional.

With this in mind, think about items you'd like to bring into your life in the future. Let's break it down and give you a little more accountability and understanding about why you want these items and if you **really** need them.

What is it?	Why do you want it?	What stores have you found it in?	When will you buy it?

Mindful Consumption

The biggest thing we can learn from our elders is to do less and enjoy the simple things more. I can often find my Nannan just sitting in her chair looking out of the window watching the world go by. If I accidentally interrupt her she'll say "Oh I was in a world of my own then!". What a wonderful place to be. This peace and stillness is something I feel the younger generations are going to lose over time if importance isn't placed on it.

Close your eyes and think deeply, when was the last time you just sat and watched the world go by?

_____

_____

_____

Where were you? How did you feel?

_____

_____

_____

The benefits of living intentionally

*So much good comes when you are truly living
in each moment*

I really started to lean into slow living more when I started struggling with chronic fatigue. I was doing too much. Working too many hours. Wearing far too many hats! I was a hard worker, working 40+ hours a week at some points. I was a girlfriend, trying to be a present daughter, a non-flaky friend, a good granddaughter, a carer to my dad and all the while trying to nurture my online community that I'd spent so many years finding. I was frazzled to say the least and I had no time left for *me*.

My body gave up on me. It forced me to slow down, to stop.

I was no longer able to do everything I had once done. I struggled with normal daily tasks, feeling too tired and too drained. It completely changed my outlook on life and made me reevaluate who I was and why I was working so many hours.

Was it worth my sanity? When the time came that I could reduce my hours I did it in a heartbeat I didn't care about the pay cut, I'd make it work somehow. I needed more time to heal and just live.

Do you work too many hours in a week? Ask yourself why do you work overtime? Do you do it to buy nice things or maybe it's for nice experiences for yourself and loved ones. Do you do it because your current lifestyle is set up for it and without that overtime you wouldn't have enough money at the end of the month? For some people working overtime is a necessity and essential to make ends meet and not a lifestyle choice.

What can you do differently here? Can you work fewer hours and get to enjoy life more? Would working less have a positive impact on you and your loved ones? Is there any way you can make some money on the side with a passion you have? Crafting, babysitting, cooking, selling unwanted items etc. The less pressure you have to work overtime the less stressful your life will be.

Sometimes in life we need a wake up call but you don't have to wait until you hit rock bottom to get started.

I don't say no
because I am so busy,
I say no because
I don't want to be
so busy.

Courtney Carver

The benefits of leading a more intentional life -

You start to appreciate your time

As I mentioned earlier, time is valuable and being intentional with what you do with it will change your life. Honoring your time is the most impactful thing you'll ever do. Time is an energy exchange. We all know the phrase 'time is money' but it really is true. If you start to think about the cost of an item being the amount of time it would take you to earn that money you will start to realise the true value of what you spend your money on. You will be less impulsive and less willing to waste your time or the money you earned with that time.

You become more present & connected

When you're more present, you value your life more and the experiences you have. You're able to really live in the moment more and you will thank yourself later down the line. Memories will be so much clearer and how you felt at the time will be too. Taking time to reflect on your days will allow you to process all that happened, meaning you will be able to recall it better later on.

If anything negative happens it means you're going to spend time processing this now rather than suppressing it and it coming up later on in life. Not only this but the memories you make and the life you experience will be so much better because you will be connecting more and living in the moment rather than just existing.

Less stress

One of the main reasons I think people come to feel called to the slow living lifestyle is to find more peace and in turn, less stress. Running around at 100mph all the time is exhausting and anxiety inducing. There is no worse feeling (in my life) than flipping over to a new month on your calendar and nearly every day having writing on! Fewer commitments = less stress. Less stress = less pressure. Less pressure = more happiness and that means much more brain-space for existing and enjoying life!

Intentionality trickles into every single area of your life

As you walk this new path of intentional living you'll find yourself questioning everything you do, consume, buy, wear etc. Over time you will start to curate the slow and simple life you've always dreamed of. One day you'll look back and realise the amount of last minute rushed decisions you've made has lessened and in turn your life is so much more organised and *intentional.*

You'll be proud of the path you've been on and will be able to look back and reflect on how much better you now feel.

More happiness

It goes without saying that the biggest benefit to living a more intentional life is that you will find greater happiness in everyday life and in turn enjoy a more balanced and present existence. If you find lots of small things that make you happy each day they will start to add up, which is much better than draining your cup and occasionally filling it with that one 'big thing'. Those big things are fleeting and few and far between but the little things are always there, you just have to look for them.

You learn to appreciate the little things in life

Leading on from my last point you will realise that there are so many tiny little things that happen each day that can put a smile on your face or give you a sense of calm/wholeness. It could be the sunrise, a hot cup of coffee warming your hands, cuddling with loved ones or pets, breathing in fresh air, seeing spider webs in the morning dew, looking forward to the end of a day and putting your favourite pjs on... there are so many things to look out for and be grateful for and they change each day.

Core Values

a simple guide to finding out
what matters to you most

Now you know the foundations of a simple life you need to find your own personal values. These are at the core of everything and are the most important part of your entire journey. It's important to remember that your core values can change over time and there is no reason to feel guilty about this, just walk along your path with your head held high no matter what.

It's important to understand what core values are so that you can start to figure out what your own personal ones are. We all hold values but sometimes we're not actually aware of them. This is where problems can start to arise. If you don't sit down and tune into your own psyche to find out your values, it's really easy to act out of line of what you feel is 'right' and that can cause a lot of confusing feelings and emotional turmoil.

There are many benefits to finding and following your own core values. Personal values highlight what you stand for: if you stand firm in your beliefs you will gain confidence in yourself and have a greater sense of fulfilment in daily life. They also represent your unique and individual self. No two people's values are exactly identical, they are what makes you, *you.*

So here is how you find your own personal core values.

Experience

What have you experienced so far in life that has stood out for you, good or bad? Big life changes like quitting a job, getting a promotion, a personal or family tragedy, giving birth, writing a book...

Think deeply about all that has created you into the person you are today. Dig into every nook and cranny really trying to think of all the times you were at a crossroads in your life and had to choose which way to turn.

What did you feel at that moment? How did that moment shape you into who you are today?

What values did you hold at that moment in time? Did these values help or hinder you?

Take a moment to make some notes below about your own personal life changing experiences

Experience	How did you feel at that moment?	How did it change your life and shape you into who you are today?	What values did you hold at that time?	Did these values help or hinder you?

Compare

When looking at your big life experiences, compare the good with the bad. What did you learn from these experiences? What were you proud of, do you feel you could have handled the situation better?

Experience	What did you learn?	What were you proud of?	How could you handle it better if it happened again?

Now, for each experience write one word that summarises it. Make it a positive word. If the experience didn't go to plan what do you wish had happened? What would you do differently and what word would you then write? For example, loyalty, drive, focus, passion, kindness, caring, loving.

Experience 1 Word
To describe:

_____

Experience 2 Word
To describe:

_____

Experience 3 Word
To describe:

_____

The words you just chose are the values you held or gained from the experience you had.

Now for each value, score it out of 5 based on how much this word resonates with you (1 being the least , 5 being most).

Value 1
Score -

Value 2
Score -

Value 3
Score -

Now write a little list of words you feel resonate with you now. I will share a list of words to help you along, pick out the ones that stand out the most to you.

Kind
Inspiring
Loving
Determined
Loyal
Courageous
Generous
Authentic
Graceful
Charitable
Hard Working
Honest
Reliable
Disciplined
Fierce
Relaxed
Accepting
Enthusiastic
Organised
Patient
Genuine
Gentle
Devoted
Compassionate
Passionate
Fun
Calm
Adaptable
Motivated
Spontaneous

Value 1

_____

Value 2

_____

Value 3

_____

Value 4

_____

Value 5

_____

You now have your personal values; you know inside how these values make you feel. Try to live in alignment with these words. Take a moment to sit with each of the values you chose and write a few feelings that come up. Your logical brain may try to take over here. I often do this exercise with my clients and find people struggle to 'feel' and instead try to process.

E.g

Value 1: Kindness

How does it make you feel? Warm. Happy. Loved

Value 2: Determined

How does it make you feel? Powerful. Assured. Happy.

Now it's your turn

Value 1:

How does it make you feel?

_____

Value 2:

How does it make you feel?

_____

Value 3:

How does it make you feel?

_____

Value 4:

How does it make you feel?

Value 5:

How does it make you feel?

Write your values down and put them on your mirror, fridge or your phone lock screen. Anywhere you will see them. Having a constant visual reminder of the values you have or want to work towards will help you to stay on the right path towards your dream life.

Small choices make big change -

Those every day decisions really count.
Here's how to choose them wisely

I've already touched on this topic slightly in the chapter "Wisdom from our elders" but I feel there is still lots to speak about on this topic. It's easy to forget but every single day we make countless choices. In fact, some sources suggest that we make as many as 35,000 choices every single day. [2]

I feel exhausted just reading that number! We spend at least 7-8 hours asleep so all of those choices are made in our waking hours which equates to about 2000 decisions per hour or a decision every 2 seconds! [3]

Decision fatigue is real and it is a big problem. It can cause you to feel incapable of making even the smallest decision and can cause huge overwhelm in daily life. Some people even feel paralysed and start stalling in life. They stall because they intentionally avoid making any decisions because the commitment to do so feels way too much.

The thing is, some of these tiny choices don't need to be made every single day, some you can bulk together and decide at the start of the week. Simple tools such as keeping a calendar for appointments and events, creating a weekly meal plan or batch cooking meals and storing them in the freezer can help to reduce that daily feeling of overwhelm.

You may have heard about Mark Zuckerberg and other highly successful people having a daily uniform that is always the same. An entire wardrobe of identical socks, t-shirts, trousers and underwear. Taking the decision out of such a simple but mundane thing as what to wear really helps to lessen the amount of brain activity you use each day on such a menial thing. I'm not personally a fan of having such a strict and rigid 'uniform'. I like to express myself through clothing but I can appreciate how having one less decision to make each day would create much more brain space for other, more important things.

If you're like me and you enjoy having a varied wardrobe, think about creating a capsule wardrobe. A capsule wardrobe is intentionally selected pieces chosen for their style, colour and ability to look nice with other items in your wardrobe. Many items work well together which means you can make multiple outfits out of the same few items. This results in you needing fewer clothes overall as the items you own are much more versatile.

There are countless resources out there for creating the perfect year-round or seasonal capsule wardrobe. However, if you're already feeling overwhelmed, the idea of completely revamping your wardrobe may be a step too far.

Here's what to do instead. A simple but effective tool I've used for years now is having a colour palette. For me that is beige, white, olive green and dusky pink, you can see it all through my home, the clothes I wear and my own branding colours on my website and Instagram feed. You may already know your colour preferences, but if you're not sure what yours are, have a look around your home. What colours stand out the most? What colours were the last 5 pieces of clothing you bought? You will start to notice a theme.

Top 3 colours you feel drawn to

1.

2.

3.

I personally go through phases in my life where I'm drawn to certain colours and I like to embrace them fully and move and flow as I go. That means sometimes there are times where my entire wardrobe no longer feels 'right' and I slowly start to change it to fit with who I'm becoming.

Honoring this has been life changing for me: it's helped me to accept that I am always changing and growing. Realising that I will never be 'perfect' and I will never have a 'perfect' wardrobe helps me to have space to blossom and grow outside of the box I feel society tends to put us in.

I believe we're drawn to certain colours at certain times in our lives and honoring that can really help you to feel positive and confident. Below is a list of popular colours and their own individual meanings:

White - *Purity, Cleanliness, Peace*
Beige - *Neutral, Calm, Relaxing*
Black - Mystery, Masculinity, Passion
Red - *Passion, Courage, Love*
Yellow - *Happiness, Hope, Joy*
Pink - *Love, Femininity, Kindness*
Green - *Abundance, Grounding, Fresh*
Purple - *Creativity, Royalty, Wealth*
Orange - *Energy, Happiness, Vitality*
Blue - *Calm, Sadness, Imagination*

Research for yourself your own list of colours and see if you can find deeper meaning in the ones you feel drawn to. What do they represent? How do you feel when you wear them?

Once you have your list of colours, have a look at a colour chart and start to think of ways you can make your wardrobe fit your current sense of style whilst also avoiding clashing colours.

I tend to be drawn to neutrals which makes my wardrobe very easy to coordinate but you may be drawn to bold colours and that can work too. Be sure you have an array of colour options for both tops and bottoms and you'll never be stuck for what to wear.

Limit your options

One of the things that gets me down each week is thinking of what meals to make and writing a shopping list. A family member of mine once told me a really great way to conquer this. Write down all of the meals you and your family enjoy onto little pieces of paper and pop them into a jar. Before you go to the shop pull out 7 pieces of paper and there you have this week's meal plan. Meals you already know how to make and now you don't have to make 7 separate decisions, easy! You could go one step further if you have the time, create a meal plan for the entire week, including all meals. This way there is no question about what you're eating that week and the best part? Little to no food waste! It is hard to begin with but over time it gets easier to know what meals to decide on. I also like to keep a rolling shopping list on my phone with tick boxes (I just use the iPhone notes app).

When I'm planning meals I also write a shopping list and check my kitchen for what I already have. I make a list of every item I need to buy and try not to deviate from it.

My list is split into categories and they are in order of how they appear in the supermarket I personally use each week.

1. Fruit & Veg
2. Dairy
3. Meat & Fish
4. Eggs
5. Cupboard foods
6. Frozen
7. Bakery
8. Household/Other

Each week I just untick everything in the list from last week then add and change things to fit my new weekly menu. Ordinary things like milk, eggs, onions etc just stay there and it makes it a really quick and easy job.

As I walk around the store, I sometimes find myself picking up something extra I don't need or deciding on a different meal for the week. Ideas like this popping up and taking over our original plans can actually be a form of self-sabotage. If you decide to throw away your meal plan and opt for the new exciting ideas you've found in the supermarket, you are not honoring the time it took you that morning to sit down and think of seven meal ideas for the week. That being said, don't let these inspired meal ideas escape you, write them down for another time or for next week's menu. But also, don't let them deviate you from the path that you're already on.

Set Deadlines

If you have trouble making decisions, big or small, one easy trick is to give yourself a deadline. That may be a week or just until the end of the day. If you're really having trouble committing to something, ask yourself why. Sit with this for a while and ask if it's really serving you or why you're holding yourself back from committing?

Decision to be made	Why are you holding back	Deadline to complete by

Now you have tools to reduce decision fatigue in daily life, it's important to state here that all these little decisions each day that add up to create your **life** and your **future**. Addressing decision fatigue is one of the fastest ways to change your life. If you suffer with decision fatigue you will find you stop making conscious decisions, you also stop being a conscious creator in your life and it's easy to start to drift.

Imagine how easy it is to drift out to sea on a Lilo. You're gazing at the clouds, enjoying the sunshine, all responsibilities were left on the beach and you're completely oblivious of the world around you. Suddenly reality hits you and you sit up and realise how far you are from the shore. Panic sets in… But it's never too late to start swimming back to shore.

I'm giving you a life raft. Here, **get in**!

Let's get you back to the shore, back to a life of intention where every decision you make is impactful and meaningful.

The Art Of Living

The number one aspect of life you really need to
focus on to create a more peaceful, less stressful life

Your thoughts are what make you, you. Every thought
you've ever had has created the version of you that is
right here reading this book. Some thoughts we act
upon, some we don't. Some we let fester, others we let
go. Not all thoughts are created equally and not all
thoughts serve us.

Being aware of your thoughts will change your life
faster than you even knew was possible. I've already
mentioned how powerful mindfulness is and what an
amazing impact it can have on your daily life and I felt
it important to mention here that *your everyday
thoughts are no different.*

Have you ever noticed how quickly your mood can
change when you receive a negative comment,
message or experience?

It could be the best day in the world but one thing gets said and a big dark cloud comes over you. The words are loaded and you're triggered. You obsess over it, the words or experience whirl around in your head on repeat as you try to make sense of it.

All of your focus has gone on to the negative experience.

You are focusing on something negative and also something out of your control.

What will happen next? Does any good come when you're in a bad mood? Usually people in a bad mood will be snappy, mean, short tempered and emotional. You're now taking all of that into your day *with you.*

Have you ever had a bad day that just kept getting worse? You can't believe how the day turned out and you find yourself ranting about the terrible series of events that happened that day to a loved one "and then this! And can you believe it, then this! And on top of that...!" There is usually a final straw before you completely explode into hysterics and rightly so. That much negativity is no good for anything. You bring more of what you focus on into your day. Focus on the bad? You will see and experience *more* bad. There are days when you are in an amazing mood and nothing can get in your way but then something awful happens and turns it upside down. Some things we aren't in control of but we are in control of how we respond to them.

If you find yourself in a whirlwind of bad things happening and a bad day unfolding, stop and take a breath. Remind yourself that it's ok and that you will get through it. That being angry about it won't help, it will only give it more energy.

It's easy to become focused on the negatives of everyday life - so many little things can go wrong on any given day. They can also go catastrophically wrong on a big important day. We've all heard stories of brides in hysterics on their wedding day (the term bridezilla wasn't created by accident!) When you focus all of your attention on things you can't control it's very easy to start to feel *out* of control. Before you know it, external experiences are controlling your emotions and in turn, your life.

Instead, focus on the good. Set your mind to scan for the positives: scan for hope and faith.

At the end of each day while you're laying in bed, think about your day. As you do, no doubt you will think of all you didn't achieve, what went wrong and what you need to do better tomorrow. Quieten those thoughts and turn your attention to the good.

What good happened today? What are you proud of? What small thing put a smile on your face today?

True happiness and peace comes from the simple little moments in daily life and the more you look for them the more you will find.

Imagine the last time you had a good day. Why was it good? What made it so much better than the rest? Were you happy on this day?

When you're in a good mood you see all the good things around you. If I go on a walk in a good mood I see people smiling, kids playing and laughing, running around in the playground. I see cute ducks on a pond and their ducklings swimming after them. I see the leaves changing colour on the trees and bees buzzing past, busy with their day. I notice more. I see more. The more good I see the better I feel and the cycle continues on.

Start to foster deep gratitude for your life. Find time to celebrate the fact you're here today and you get to have an entire new day tomorrow. You have goals, dreams and desires and nothing in the world is going to stop you.

All you need is determination to keep trying and to keep showing up, day in, day out. It's easy to take life for granted but the more you remember how special it is and how honored you are to be here the more grateful you will become.

A simple guide to decluttering

Not sure where to start? Start here

Clutter is chaos. Plain and simple!

Nobody enjoys living in chaos. Chaos can enter our lives for lots of reasons. Sometimes life gets to be too much and you start to de-prioritise your values. You find yourself buying things to fill a void. You run out of time to keep your home tidy. Your schedule becomes overwhelming and you start missing appointments and important dates.

Getting your life back in order can feel like a mammoth task and it is if you try to do everything all in one go. Instead let's break it down into different sections. I believe there to be four types of clutter:

1. Physical Clutter
2. Digital Clutter
3. Mental Clutter
4. Emotional Clutter

Physical clutter

This is the 'stuff' we bring into our lives. Some of the items we own serve us and others don't. There are some really extreme minimalists in the world whose entire worldly possessions fit into one backpack. I'm forever in awe of those people! Personally, it's not a lifestyle I would enjoy.

I know that first hand as I have lived out of a backpack and I found it liberating but quite unfulfilling. I know now I'm a homebody. I find comfort in having a cosy familiar environment and for me that means nice fluffy blankets, pictures of my family, a few intentionally selected decor pieces and lots of pillows!

Decluttering isn't one size fits all, it's different for every single person. All that matters is that your version works for you.

If you own items that you're unsure about, ask yourself would you pay to keep it in storage? If the answer is no, you know what to do. If you feel conflicted about removing items from your life at the start, put them into a box and keep it to one side for a set amount of time. It can give you a feeling of reassurance when you're first getting started with decluttering but I assure you it **does** get easier to let go of items as time goes on.

Digital clutter

Once you've decluttered your physical life, digital declutter is next on the list! This one is a weak spot for me personally. I have so many pictures. I'm definitely guilty of taking pictures and then never looking through them or even looking at them again! I keep multiples of the same pictures and forget to delete the ones I don't need. I've known my picture album on my phone have 12,000 photos and I *still* felt resistant to delete any! This resistance is also a form of overwhelm.

Who really wants to sit and look through 12,000 pictures and try to decide which to delete? Not me. But it needs to be done at some point. The thing is, you don't have to delete your memories. I remind myself of that often. If you enjoy looking back through those memories there is no shame in that. Instead, try to set yourself a goal of deleting any duplicates- maybe spend 5 minutes a day just going through and deleting any that you took that week that you no longer need. Any you want to keep, move to a digital storage space in an organised folder. That way your photos are not only decluttered but organised too.

Organising your emails, work files and important documents is key to keeping you sane! Folders are your best friend. Make folders within folders within folders, date everything and make sure you describe what each folder is.

It will make it easier to find again in the future. This is an opportunity to develop accountability. Hold yourself accountable to creating and using the folders you create. It will not only make life easier but it will streamline that area of your life too.

Mental clutter

This is the stuff we hold onto that doesn't matter. It's the million appointments and obligations we have flying around in our brain making us feel busy and overwhelmed. It's everything you think of as you close your eyes to go to sleep at night. Make use of this clutter and **write it down**.

Stop it from causing chaos by putting it in its place. Put it in a list, give it somewhere to go, something to do. It's there for a reason. Stop letting it get in your way and start holding yourself accountable to creating lists and dealing with them one tick at a time.

Emotional Clutter

This is one of the hardest forms of clutter to deal with. It's the stuff that holds people back in life. It's limited thinking... poor self worth... Unresolved trauma. Toxic relationships. Bad habits.

You may find when you're decluttering other areas of your life that strong emotions come up and leave you feeling overwhelmed and miserable. Usually that is a sign that there is something coming up for you that needs acknowledging.

What are you feeling? What caused that feeling? What were you doing that caused it?

Sitting with your feelings is one of the most powerful things you can do. You may find you instantly try to limit the pain by defaulting to one of your many coping mechanisms but try to stop yourself. Coping mechanisms are different for each person but some examples are: scrolling endlessly on your phone, opening the fridge and seeing what you could eat to distract yourself, getting up and making another cup of tea or watching mindless TV in order to fill your brain with noise. Instead, lean into the discomfort. See what comes up for you. Don't push yourself too hard with this but do try to untangle your thoughts and feelings. Try journaling and writing down how you feel. It will help you to get a better understanding of what is happening and I usually find with journaling that by the time you're finished writing you've already rationalised the problem and found a way to help yourself to cope with it.

If you find yourself struggling to cope with processing your thoughts and feelings by journaling it is a good idea to speak to a therapist and find ways to cope with the feelings or memories that you're experiencing.

One of my favourite journaling activities is called 'a page a day'. It's as simple as it sounds. Each day sit down and write an entire page of your notebook. If at the start you're not sure what to write, just write about not knowing what to write and as you start writing the words will come. You might even surprise yourself with what comes up. Worries, stresses, excitement, deadlines, conversations. All of these are things that are lingering in your subconscious mind, floating around causing chaos in your thoughts.

Score yourself out of 10 (10 being most cluttered) for how cluttered these areas of your life are.

Physical clutter: /10
Digital clutter: /10
Mental clutter: /10
Emotional Clutter: /10

Now you know what area(s) you need to focus on first. If all areas are 10/10 and you're not sure where to start, start with physical clutter and work your way down the list. I found personally that once I started to remove physical clutter from my life, the decluttering process started trickling into all areas of my life. Once you have one area sorted start to move to the next, that way you won't overwhelm yourself.

A word of warning here. Decluttering can easily be turned into an obsession. It can become a way for you to unwind and be in control of something.

If you start to feel yourself becoming too controlling about what you own and how your home looks, take a step back for a while. If you feel resistance from that it could be time to speak to a professional and get some help. There is never any shame in seeking help, after all it will help to get you back on track.

With physical clutter start room by room, writing a list of which areas you want to tackle first. In each room write down what parts of the room feel most overwhelming and do those first. For example, when I first started my decluttering journey my bedroom was the first place I started. I started with my wardrobe. It felt familiar but it was also bursting at the seams. There weren't many really strong emotions for me when it came to saying goodbye to clothing so it was quite a nice way to ease into it. The next area was my chest of drawers- they were absolute chaos! They were so bad. I couldn't even open the drawers. Each time I decluttered an area, I dealt with what I no longer needed straight away. I put it all into bags and it went straight into my car ready to go to the charity store or the tip. After that, I caught the bug. It was really rewarding having more organisation in my life and the more I decluttered, the better I felt.

Though you might have decluttered your entire home you may find that occasionally going through areas of your home can be helpful. Possessions starts to accumulate over time. Things you once used and loved but no longer do. Be intentional with what you own and check in with your items from time to time.

Habit stacking

An easy and helpful guide
to creating new habits

This is my number one minimalist hack. I'd never heard of it until a few years ago. I think when trying to create a new routine, it's something many of us have tried in the past, be that consciously or unconsciously. The problem starts when we overwhelm ourselves with a new routine that is so very different from our current one.

Unfamiliar new routines are notoriously really hard to keep. There's a study[4] that shows it takes 66 days for a new habit to become automatic, meaning you no longer think about it, you just do it like you would get out of bed or turn off a light. You no longer second guess yourself or attach any thought to it, you just do it.

We all have a lot of habits, some we are aware of and some we are not. One thing I think we can all agree on is how hard it is to create habits and actually stick to them for long enough that they make a difference in our lives.

But what is a habit?

A habit is a routine or behavior that is repeated regularly and tends to occur subconsciously.[5] One of the worst habits most children and some adults have? Biting fingernails. It's a subconscious habit, maybe even a nervous habit that brings comfort.

At some point awareness is brought to this habit - society tends to frown upon it - and you decide you no longer want to do it. Each time you do that habit you then stop yourself. It takes a long time but eventually you get there. For some a reminder is needed. There is a bitter tasting nail polish that a friend of mine once used and it worked. It tasted so disgusting that she couldn't put her fingers anywhere near her mouth! It worked really well for her and helped to derail that habit.

So now let's talk about habits in relation to daily routines. Good habits are ones that help you move forward in life, be it for mental health, physical wellbeing or habits that set you up for a good and productive day. Bad habits tend to hold you back: they might be the easier option or even an option that doesn't actually fit with your own personal morals.

Examples of habits:

Good Habits	Bad Habits
Brushing Teeth	Using a snooze alarm
Making Bed	Forgetting to write down appointments
Getting up on first alarm	Skipping breakfast or eating something unhealthy on the way to work.
Eating a healthy breakfast	Drinking coffee instead of eating a meal
Drinking 2L water a day	Not putting clothes away
Choosing clothes the day before	Forgetting to open curtains or make the bed

Transforming the 'bad' habits into 'good' ones:

Bad Habits	Good Habits
Using a snooze alarm	Getting up on first alarm
Not leaving enough time to make the bed	Making bed and opening the curtains in a morning
Skipping breakfast or eating something unhealthy on the way to work	Planning meals ahead of time and meal prepping so you're not in a rush and can maintain a balanced, healthy diet
Drinking coffee instead of drinking water	Drinking 2L water a day and tracking consumption it to make sure
Trying on 5 different outfits in a morning and having to leave a messy bedroom behind as you don't have time to put them all away again	Choosing clothes the day before so you're ready and prepared the next morning
Forgetting to go to appointments and letting people down	Using a calendar to schedule all appointments and setting reminders so you never forget.

Each person's good and bad habits will be wildly different, so write your own list of habits that you currently have, both good and bad. For any bad habits you can think of, see if you can turn it into a good habit going forwards.

Good Habits	Bad Habits

Habit stacking is the simple practise of stacking good habits on top of each other and not leaving space for the ones that you want to remove. These new 'good' habits then become automatic and over time your brain stops needing to think about them and they start to become part of your normal daily routine. Ever wondered how people who win marathons manage to get out and run every day? They don't accidentally win those races; they work towards that medal every single day. They set their focus and build their days for success. They make running an everyday habit and they prioritise it.

A lot of people thrive on chaos without realising it but chaos is destructive and unproductive. It hinders rather than helps. Society tends to show routine and structure as robotic and unattainable but that is far from the truth. Instead, allow yourself the opportunity to commit to new habits and stick at them for long enough to see the changes they create within your life.

My family dog, Murphie, loved routine. He thrived with routine! So much so that he would come and sit with puppy dog eyes just before he knew it was time for his dinner. How did he know it was time? Routine.

He had social queues that he waited for and he knew it was time. He did the same in the evening. He'd get up and put himself to bed at 10pm every night because my mum has always been amazing at keeping routine in her life. She goes to bed at 10pm most nights unless there is a specific reason for her not to.

It's not about being too rigid and leaving no room for spontaneity but allowing yourself the freedom to experience new and useful routines. Something that if you don't already do, may just change your life.

I truly believe that the key to a successful morning is actually in the evening before. There are lots of morning routine videos on YouTube about people getting up at 5 or 6am but not many share what time they go to sleep at night and how they get a good night's rest.

I recently committed to getting up at 6am every day. So far I've been doing it for just over a month and it's changed my entire routine, for the better. It doesn't matter what time I go to bed; I get up with my alarm at 6am every day except Sunday. I treasure Sundays; they are my relaxing day so no alarm. But do you know what is funny?

On Sundays I wake up naturally at about 7:30am whereas before I would wake at 9am. What a difference it makes to my days. I have so much more time to enjoy life! I find I'm actually tired at bed time and I've naturally started winding down for bed at about 9:30pm and I'm usually asleep before 11pm.

In the past I would stay up until past midnight doing nothing in particular and then get up really late the next day. That lateness would chase me all day long and keep me up way past my bedtime as I felt I was missing out if I went to bed early.

It's just a simple shift in perspective. I still get the same amount of work time and leisure time, they're just at more sociable and productive times of day now! I no longer feel like my days are running away without me. If you don't already get up at a certain time each day, try it for a week and see how it goes. I hope it is as profound for you as it has been for me.

Here's a list of what I personally believe to be good habits for winding down after a long day and setting the next day up for success.

Eating a nutritious meal
Going for a slow leisurely walk for 15-20 minutes to help you digest
Drinking a cup of chamomile tea (or herbal tea that aids sleep) before bed
Catching up with social media and watching your favourite programmes in a time dedicated to this, let
your brain switch off for a little while
Brushing your teeth
Having a skin care routine
Dimming the lights in your bedroom
Drawing the curtains and creating a nice ambiance
Setting your alarm and phone in aeroplane mode
Winding down in bed with a fiction book
A 5-10 minute mindfulness meditation of breathwork practise.
Going to bed in time to get at least 7/8 hours of sleep.

What would a peaceful and wholesome evening look like for you?

On this list, put a * next to any habits you already have in your daily routine, this will help you to find anchors to fix your new habits onto.

To successfully create a new routine you want to stack new habits on top of old existing habits. When you stack a new habit under an old existing one, your brain starts to associate the two. The old habit acts as a trampoline leading you to performing the new one. The more times you do the two in sequence the easier it becomes to replicate and in turn the easier it is to set up a new routine and start adding more positive habits into your routine.

Find a new habit you want to start, for example: reading, listening to podcasts, walking, running, brushing teeth, opening curtains in morning. Find a habit you already automatically do and could use as an anchor for your new habit. These are usually really simple, it could be things like getting into bed, getting dressed, turning on a light, drinking water etc.

Group your habits together and make them sequential. Look at your list of good habits from earlier and find crossover points where you could stack a new habit between. You can then start to build entire chains of habits. It takes time to create long sequences of new habits but over time you can start adding more and more. When your brain carries out an automatic habit the only thing it then has to remember is what comes next. Essentially, you're playing dot-to-dot, but knowing what the dots are drawing makes it easier for you to connect them. The human brain thrives with sequence, routine and predictability.

Here is an example of a list of anchor habits and how I've stacked new habits under each. Occasionally there will be a habit you already have that could be improved, e.g. Eating a meal could be improved by making it more nutritious. This isn't necessarily a new habit, but an optimised old one.

Anchor Habit	**New Habit**
Eat a meal	(Make it nutritious)
	Go for a walk to digest
Turn downstairs lights on	
	Switch kettle on and make a nice cup of tea
Catch up with social media on sofa	(decide how long you will be on your phone for so you don't lose your entire night scrolling!)
Go upstairs and brush teeth	
	Make time to do skincare routine
Dim lights in bedroom	
	Draw curtains and light candles
Get into bed	
	Set alarm, switch phone to aeroplane mode

Wind down in bed (not on phone)	
	Read a book
Put book away,	
	Mediate for 5-10 mins
Turn off light & blow out candles	
Go to sleep	

With this series of habits there is a starting point to create a much more refined and purposeful routine.

New Routine
Eat a nutritious meal
Go for a walk to digest
Turn the downstairs lights on
Switch the kettle on and make a nice cup of tea
Sit on the sofa and set a timer for the amount of time you want to spend catching up on social media.
Go upstairs and brush teeth
Skincare routine
Dim lights in bedroom
Draw curtains and light candles
Get into bed
Set alarm, switch phone to aeroplane mode
Wind down in bed
Read a book
Put book away
Meditate for 5-10 minutes
Turn off lights & blow out candles
Go to sleep

Look at your current list of habits from the earlier exercise and try to think of ways you can implement new ones into the list you just created.

New List

Anchor Habit	New Habit

New Routine

Ask Yourself Why

Why do you want to do these new habits? *Why?* Is always a really important question to ask.

Taking the time to clearly state the impact of new habits is key to remembering why you started it in the first place. People usually start new habits because they believe they are going to have a really positive impact on their lives which is a great and positive thing to want but let's face it, there will be bumps in the road. Life is never completely plain sailing and so being able to reflect on your why is going to be helpful at times when you feel like giving up and going back to your old, much easier routine.

*What is your **why**?*

_____

_____

_____

_____

_____

_____

_____

Hold yourself accountable
The importance of accountability

Have you ever felt really inspired and full of enthusiasm after planning your future and setting yourself some big life changing goals? You're going to change your life and it all starts **tomorrow**. Tomorrow you will get up early! Tomorrow you will get up on your first alarm and seize the day.

Tomorrow comes, the alarm goes off. You grumble at your alarm, roll over and go straight back to sleep.
You're in a completely different mindset to what you were in yesterday but the problem here is that you're in a really bad habit routine. You can have all of the energy you had last night in the morning; you just have to remember **why** you want to get up early.

Maybe you do the opposite. You jump out of bed with enthusiasm, excited to take on the day with every intention to keep up with this new healthy habit for the rest of the week. But the next day comes, your alarm goes off and you think "I'm really tired. I have to have balance in life. Sleep is important. I'll get up early tomorrow..."

Just like that, you lost all of your momentum. Accountability out of the window. All self-trust crumbled to dust. It seemed like such a quick, simple decision at the time but what you don't realise is, each time you go back on your words like that, you're diminishing the trust you have in yourself.

Imagine if you had a friend who just kept letting you down. Over and over again. How would you feel? Would you want to keep being friends with them when they didn't show up at the time they said? If they kept disappointing you?

If you wouldn't do this to a friend or allow a friend to do this to you stop and ask yourself why. Next time you find yourself letting yourself down or going back on a promise you made to yourself, take a moment to remember how big of an impact that decision is going to have on your own self accountability and personal worth.

It's important to remember you're not alone in this. It is human design and there are many reasons you can struggle to hold yourself accountable. Understanding what they are will help you get ahead and stop it from holding you back in life.

Lack of pressure

Without some pressure it can be hard to stay determined to meet your goals. If you have no timeline or deadlines there is no real reason to push yourself at all. You can let yourself off the hook really easily and although no pressure feels amazing, it doesn't get you very far in life. Especially when it comes to changing your habits and in turn your life. Growth comes from even the smallest amount of discomfort. It grows character and is what I like to call 'grit' for life.

There's a reason some of the most successful people in the world came from a challenging past. They had a pressure to succeed, to make anything possible. They had a strong reason why and they did what they needed to get to where they wanted to be. Without that pressure within themselves they wouldn't have had any willpower to try at all.

Too much pressure

While having no pressure is bad, having too much can also be harmful. Some people thrive on pressure and deadlines while others implode. Instead of pressure motivating you it actually harms your progress by making you feel completely overwhelmed and filled with anxiety.

Instead of focusing on one task at a time you look at everything all in one go and then decide you can do **none** of it!

You put it to one side and say, "It's all just too much". I'm sure we all know someone exactly like this from school or university. There is always someone who is a crammer. They wait until the very last minute to get an entire essay written in one night. The pressure finally boils to a head and they have no choice but to do it all there and then! They stay up all night long to get it done or maybe they just can't and they have to ask for an extension on their deadline. The problem with this is the amount of pressure hasn't changed. All that is happening is you have been ignoring and burying the pressure and pretending it doesn't exist.

The deadline was there all along. The word count didn't change. You still need to do the work. Putting it off doesn't achieve anything. It needs dealing with, not hiding from. If the pressure is too much, lessen it until it feels less overwhelming. Break it down into smaller, more achievable sections. Give yourself longer deadlines or shorter tasks that are easier to reach. Rather than trying to write an entire book in one week, try and write a few pages per day. Having that small sense of self-satisfaction goes a long way and gives you a much needed boost of confidence along the way.

Lack of direction

Without clear direction, where are you going? Imagine a hiker setting off into the mountains without a map. Where is he going? How will he know how to navigate the terrain? How will he get home again? How will he know where he is if there are no signs to tell him where he is or how far from home he is? Walking through life with no direction is exactly like this but so many people are happy to walk this challenging path without ever realising that they have no idea where they're going! None are actually equipped to deal with the consequences.

Although having clear goals seems quite limiting and scary, trust me it's so much easier to navigate life with them by your side. If you have a clear path to success, you have check-in points and you know how far you have come and how far you have to go.

Lack of focus

Procrastination is your enemy! The brain is a clever old thing; it will do anything to avoid pain and suffering of any kind and while that can be helpful, in this instance it is quite the opposite!

As I said before, the most growth you will ever experience will happen when you're challenging yourself the most. There is no growth without change. Your brain will do anything to help you to avoid discomfort which is why it's so easy to lay in bed rather than get up early. What you don't realise at that moment is getting up early is for your greater good and that the tiredness you're feeling will help you go to bed earlier in the evening so tomorrow you don't feel as tired as you did today. It's easy to forget but keeping that thought in your mind and having a reason *why* you're doing what you're doing will help to keep your goal in mind and most importantly it will keep you moving towards it.

Now you know the reasons why accountability may have not worked for you in the past, it's time to understand why it is the true key to success in life.

You're the creator of your own reality.

If you're constantly on autopilot letting life slip through your fingers, how do you know where you are going? Be the author of your own story. Edit the script. In reality it is you who gets up every day and goes out into the world. Your actions shape your reality and that shapes the rest of your life. Have I said that enough times that it's sunk in yet? **You** create your life. It's said that you are a product of your environment, so what are you fit for?

Are you fit for laying in bed all day? Do you want to be fit for running marathons instead? What do you need to do to change that trajectory?

This example can be used across all areas of life. If your current habits and routines aren't putting you on track for reaching your goals you need to sit down and change them so that they are, remembering to hold yourself accountable to reaching those goals every single day. If not, why did you want it in the first place? Just because it's *easier* not to try doesn't mean it's better.

Avoid victim mentality

This is a harsh reality check for you. **You** create your reality. Your habits, your relationships, your hobbies, your body, your mindset, your home. If there are things in your life now that you're not happy with, you may well have created them in the first place.

Patterns run through life and until you change those patterns your life will stay the same.

What can you do differently to change the path you're on? Don't let victim mentality get in the way of you reaching your goals. If you're not happy with something in your life it is **you** who needs to change it.

For some this can be quite a triggering message as there are things in life that are indeed out of our control but we are in control of our own minds. This also means we're in control of our emotions and how we react and deal with situations that will inevitably arise. If you don't feel in control of your mind and emotions it's because you need to build trust with yourself as you would with a friend. Build that bond with yourself by honoring your goals and rewarding yourself when you reach them.

Accountability keeps you on track

It goes without saying that if you have a clear path it is easy to stick to it. Accountability works by you meeting small goals along the way to a big goal. Set yourself up for success rather than disappointment. Make sure your goals are achievable but a little challenging. It's important to get the balance right and to check in with yourself. Only you know when you're procrastinating or if you're putting too much pressure on yourself.

Gain self trust

As I mentioned earlier, holding yourself accountable builds trust within yourself. You may not realise it but you have to have expectations of yourself and hold yourself to them.

Maybe you lack self belief and you think you're going to fail if you try anything new. You start a new diet and instantly joke that by the weekend you'll be eating takeaway. Without realising it you may meet that expectation just to please your unconscious self. This is known as a self-fulfilling prophecy. It's easier to disappoint yourself than it is to stick to your new goal. You're acting unconsciously and it's a habit. You must disappoint yourself because that is all you ever do and why stop; you're good at it *and* it's the easier option? Imagine changing this and instead you must always impress yourself? You always go above and beyond the goal.

Imagine yourself as your own employer: what would they say about you right now? Would they be happy with you or would you be going on a progress report?

Take a few minutes to consider this and then write yourself an employee review.

_____

_____

_____

_____

_____

_____

Think about what you wrote. Your answer says a lot about how much you trust yourself right now and how you're doing with personal accountability. If you found what you wrote to be quite negative, let's reframe it.

Imagine you are the best version of yourself, what does your employer say about you now?

_____

_____

_____

_____

_____

_____

_____

_____

_____

_____

_____

_____

_____

_____

_____

_____

_____

_____

_____

_____

_____

_____

The thing is, you **are** your own boss. You are the most important manager you will ever have. You manage your expectations, and you set your own goals.

Make sure you meet them.

Accountability is empowering

There is no better feeling than meeting a goal that you set. When you're first starting out with gaining accountability for yourself, even meeting the smallest goal will give you a good feeling. A feeling of deep pride. Pride builds self-belief and self-worth. It's a little cycle that goes around and each one feeds the next. Life is never linear and there will be ups and downs along the way but being able to stay on track will help to get you to where you want to be.

Accountability keeps you moving forward. Without it you will start moving sideways (getting distracted) or even backwards (losing motivation and self-belief). It keeps you aiming for the target and helps you to feel good when you meet your own expectations.

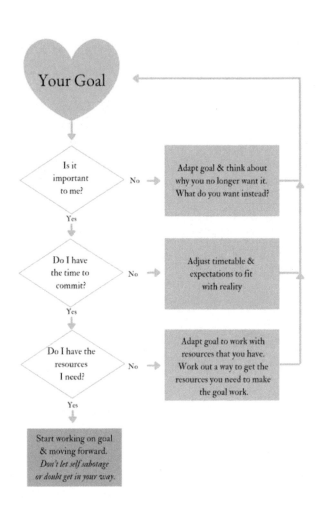

Your Goal

Is it important to me? — No → Adapt goal & think about why you no longer want it. What do you want instead?

Yes ↓

Do I have the time to commit? — No → Adjust timetable & expectations to fit with reality

Yes ↓

Do I have the resources I need? — No → Adapt goal to work with resources that you have. Work out a way to get the resources you need to make the goal work.

Yes ↓

Start working on goal & moving forward. *Don't let self sabotage or doubt get in your way.*

Create a cosy environment

Cosy stories to inspire you to create a beautiful environment and romanticise your life

Life isn't all about *doing*, even if goals are vital. We have to have balance. Life is also about being and existing. It's easy to get so caught up in daily life that we forget to look around and notice the small little changes that are quietly happening all around us. These changes happen whether we remember to notice or not. The seasons do not rely on us. They don't care if we look around and appreciate them or not, they carry on regardless, just as the world keeps on spinning and the sun keeps rising and setting, with or without an audience.

However, the seasons do have a great lesson to teach us.

They teach us to slow down. To stop and notice the beauty unfolding in each moment. It's easy to skip ahead and always live in the next moment, the next season, the next phase of life.

Winter

For those who despise winter you may feel yourself wishing it away, pining for the warmer months; resenting the warm clothes you have to wear to leave the house; scraping the ice from your car with numb fingers and enduring the dark evenings that make you feel like life is running away without you.

Winter can be hard for many reasons. It's a very harsh, polarising time of year but beauty can be found, let me assure you. As you walk to your car on a crispy, icy-cold morning stop to look closely at the trees and bushes and you will find intricate spider webs glistening with frosty morning dew. As a child I loved walking and spotting as many as I could and would often stop and stare in awe. This is a tradition my mum taught me. She once told me she would always stop to look for spider webs on her frosty morning walks to school as a child and the thought of carrying on that tradition has always made me feel warm and fuzzy.

Though the winter air is cold there is nothing more fun than breathing out cold icy breath and seeing the steam come from your mouth. Embrace your inner child and pretend to be a dragon, how big a cloud can you make? It sounds silly but these simple moments are ones that are lost as we enter adulthood.

Life doesn't always have to be so serious. I personally love wearing big cosy scarves, fluffy socks and warm cosy hats. Find the softest materials you can find and get items in your favourite colour or pattern. Create a new tradition of putting these items away with care and enjoy bringing them back out each year. Enjoy the quiet and stillness that winter brings.

Spring

Spring can be a funny season as it's the cross over from winter and into summer. The weather gets a little confused, sunny one day raining the next and it can fill people with false hope and disappointment. However, this is the month where life really flourishes. Stop to notice the blossoms starting to appear as winter fades away. Walk under a blossom tree and take a deep breath in, let the pretty scent fill you with joy. One of my favorite things to see in spring is blossoms falling gently from the trees and sweeping in a mesmerising dance across the road. Beautiful. Bees start appearing and wiggling their fuzzy bums happily as they collect nectar from the freshly bloomed flowers.

If you go for walks you will notice baby animals everywhere. Spring is the season of love and fertility in the animal kingdom and that feeling of joy and happiness is contagious. It's as if all of the plants and animals are breathing a sigh of relief and doing a little happy dance.

Summer

Summer for most is the season that is up on a pedestal. It's the hope and relief everyone has been waiting for all year. I once wished summer lasted all year long; I wanted to live in a country that stayed hot year-round. After travelling a lot, I started to really miss England. I missed home. Home for me is what is familiar and having changing seasons and endless rainy days, random week-long heatwaves and experiencing late snowfall in February and April feels like home to me and now I'm able to embrace my home country for what it is. As summer arrives it can feel like life is lighter but it can be a challenging time of year for some. Increase in social activity can be exhausting as can the change in temperature and random heat waves. Make the most of the light evenings, hot summer days, holidays and BBQ's with friends and family. I love the warm nights, sitting outside and losing track of time and the feeling of a more simple, easy to wear wardrobe at that time of year.

Autumn

You may not enjoy autumn as it's a sign that winter is approaching. You feel yourself missing the warm days and light evenings, sad to see another year drawing near.

Autumn is a personal favourite of mine, it's a relief for me that the world is starting to cool down a little. I was once a true lover of summer but as I've got older I've started to realise my introverted soul loves the colder, quieter months and there's no shame in that. Embracing this has been one of the most powerful and profound things I've ever done.

I love seeing the leaves change colour and start to fall. I find true joy in hearing the leaves crunch under my feet as I walk. Embrace the colours of autumn and bring them into your wardrobe and home. Burnt orange, warm ember red and sunshine yellow, they are all such cosy warming colours during autumn time and reflecting them will help you to feel more like you're embracing the present moment.

Some reading this may not experience extreme seasons like we do here in the UK and it's important not to compare your life to anyone else's and find yourself feeling sad or as though you're missing out. Instead find what you can love about what you experience in a year where you live and find ways to make peace with it.

Count your blessings, not your sorrows. It's ok to enjoy some months of the year more than others but one thing I've started to realise is the more I embrace the seasons, the happier I am. The more content I am. The more in the moment I am.

There is joy to find even in the darkest months and comfort to find in even the hottest of days.

There's a sunrise and a
sunset every single day,
and they're absolutely free.
Don't miss so many of them

Jo Walton

Winter

Christmas market

I can hear the sound of the music slowly getting louder as I approach the bustling market. It feels warm and comforting to be around so many others who are all here for a similar thing.

Making memories with loved ones and getting in the festive spirit. There's a gorgeous smell in the air of cinnamon and spices. I follow the smell to a stall selling mulled wine and decide to get one for myself. As the store owner pours the wine into a cute Christmas themed mug I can see the steam rising from the ladle. Warmth. I eagerly await the mug and I'm not disappointed as I take it from her. I feel the warmth radiating through my gloves warming my fingers and thumbs, I didn't realise how cold they'd gotten. As I drink the mulled wine I feel it go all the way down my throat filling my belly with warmth. My cheeks are rosy and cold but my head is warm from my cosy woolly hat. I hold the mug close to my face and let the steam warm my chilly face.

I look around and see children laughing and playing, couples hugging and holding each other close and friends arm in arm with smiles spread across their faces. Oh what a wonderful place to be.

A calm winter's night after a busy day

"Oh, what a day", I think to myself as I lock my car and walk towards my front door. Eager to leave the day behind and unwind I open the door to my home and feel a wave of ease wash over me. My cats greet me at the door, rolling around on the doormat happy to see me. I kneel down to give them a fuss and feel so grateful to have these two special souls in my life.

The house is warm from the heating that came on a few hours ago so I quickly take off my coat as I can feel myself quickly getting too hot in all of my many layers. I head upstairs and get changed into my favorite pajamas, being sure to also pop on a pair of fluffy socks and slippers. As I come back downstairs, I draw the curtains and close the day out - one of my favourite rituals during the winter. I take a few moments to light some candles and make my home feel cosy before popping the kettle on. As the water boils I feed the cats who are very excited for me to be home. They make me feel so special and loved and I take a moment to really appreciate them.

As I pour the water for my cup of tea I see the steam rise and the smell of peppermint fills the air. I grab the fuzziest blanket I can find, wrap myself up in it and jump onto the sofa. Is there any better feeling than finally sitting down after a long day? I look around and then close my eyes, taking in a big deep breath and letting all the stress from the day escape through my exhale.

Spring

A fresh Spring walk

As I walk through the woods, I notice little blossoms in the trees and glimpses of green amongst the woody branches. Little signs of re-emerging life all around. I stop and crouch down, looking closer at the remnants of an old fallen tree. It is covered in life. Fungi, lichen and insects. As I look up, I see a bee buzzing past, I follow the bee's path with my eyes and it goes to a distant flower. The flower is alone, surrounded by old decaying leaves. It has a vibrant green stem that looks strong - like nothing would stop it from growing. As I look around, I notice more and more solitary plants that have popped up. Upon getting closer I realise they are bluebells, at some point soon this entire forest floor will be covered in them, a true sign that spring is on its way.

A peaceful drive

The sky is a gorgeous dusky blue colour but closer to the ground there's a slight haze turning it from blue to white. Everything looks so pretty and pastel coloured. As I approach a farmer's field, I notice it's full of life. Calves, foals and little ducklings fill the world with joyful sound and energy. In the distance I can see a tractor busy in a field. I feel myself getting lost in my own thoughts.

It's a busy time of year for farmers who are ready to sow their seeds and get their crops ready to be harvested later in the year. Spring is all about life - the world is ready to give and live and you can feel the change of energy in the air. Hibernating animals are ready to re-emerge and the world is starting to get busier and grow louder.

As I drive through the countryside, I open my window just a crack to let some fresh air in. The air feels cool but not cold. It smells so fresh and full of life and I smile as a sense of calmness washes over me. My favorite song comes on the radio and I sing along without a care in the world, tapping my steering wheel to the beat as I drive.

Summer

A balmy summer's evening

The patio is warm from a day of sunshine and the world feels still and calm. There's the sound of quiet chatter and children's laughter echoing through the village and a lingering scent of BBQ filling the air. I take my favourite book and sit on my swing chair slowly starting to rock back and forth; one of my favorite ways to wind down on a summer evening.

The air around me feels nice, sort of like a gentle hug. I reach for my drink and hear the ice clink inside the glass as the water sloshes around. The glass has condensation from the difference in temperature and I draw a little love heart in the water and feel a little smile spread across my face. Feeling calm, peaceful and grateful for the light evenings that are here to enjoy.

Hanging the washing on a summer's day

I sit with a nice warm cup of tea patiently waiting for the washing machine to finish its last spin. The sound grows louder and louder, so loud it sounds like the machine might start moving and dance around the room, given the chance. As I wait the last few minutes for the cycle to end, I stand up and walk over to the window, looking out over my garden. I see a butterfly fluttering around near my Sweet Peas with such grace. It's easy to get lost in the beauty of nature sometimes; I feel myself letting out a gentle exhale of relief.

The washing machine clicks and there's my queue. As I open the door the delicate scent of fabric softener fills the air. I don't know if there is a more joyful scent than that on a sunny summer's day. I would once rush hanging out the laundry, such an arduously boring task. Instead, I work slowly and with intention. Paying attention to my clothes, the textures and colours. Turning them from inside out, pegging them onto the line with care.

I love seeing the washing line from inside so I hang them in a way that looks pleasing to the eye so I can keep enjoying them for the rest of the day. The sky is clear and blue, there's not a cloud in the sky. There's a gentle breeze tickling the back of my neck but it feels warm and comforting. As I peg the last item on the line I look up and see my clothes dancing around in the wind. I feel grateful that they're clean and smell nice, thankful to myself for taking the time to wash them and grateful for the sunshine that means they will be dry by the evening so I can enjoy them for the coming week.

Autumn

A crispy walk

I put on a cosy scarf and my favourite pair of boots and head out of the door. As I open the door, I feel a cool chill in the air and I'm happy to have wrapped myself up just enough but not too much. It's hard to know what to wear at this time of year, each day the temperature is a little different.

As I walk, a friendly neighbor smiles and waves. He's busy raking the leaves from his front garden. A fulltime job at this time of year and he's been busy.

There is already a pile sky high that looks just about ready to be jumped in! I enjoy the sound of the leaves crunching under my feet and intentionally walk in the thickest piles to make the most out of them being there! I love to see the different colours and shapes of the leaves and stop to take a closer look. I find a leaf that is more like a skeleton, all of the fiber has disappeared from the middle leaving just the outline of the leaf that once was. Nature never ceases to amaze me. As I look around, I notice I'm standing near a horse chestnut tree. Excitement washes over me and I run over to find the ground covered in spiky little conkers. I pick up a few and open one, revealing the gorgeous smooth conker within. I collect a few of my favorite leaves and conkers so I can bring autumn and memories of this wonderful walk back into my home too.

A day at the pumpkin patch

I wiggle my toes around in my wellington boots wishing I'd put on a different, thicker pair of socks. Why are wellies always so cold for your toes? As I approach the farm my mindset changes to gratitude as I see how muddy the field is! Now I'm glad I have them as it's rather squelchy and would be easy to lose a shoe or two here. There's a sound of laughter and children playing filling the air. Lots of families have come to pick their pumpkins for the year, as have I. As I enter the field I suddenly feel so festive and happy. Sometimes little traditions such as this can really change your mindset and get you in the festive spirit.

I kneel down and look around examining the different pumpkins. All so unique and beautiful. All to be put to use one way or another. I glance over my shoulder to see a little girl giggling and laughing as her dad wheels her around in the wheelbarrow. She's having the time of her life! Sometimes the simple things really are the best and I always feel children know the true joy of living in the moment.

As I navigate my way through the mud, stepping over pumpkin after pumpkin, I move a giant leaf and reveal a wonderful looking pumpkin. I instantly know it's coming home with me! Feeling content I pick it up and eagerly start thinking of different designs I could make on it once I'm home. I stand in line waiting to pay and can feel a buzz in the air. So many families are all here to do the same thing today, to make happy memories. As I look around I notice a little cafe off in the distance and I know for sure there is a hot chocolate in there with my name written all over it!

The seasons teach us many things but they are a consistent reminder for you to slow down.

Intentionality flows over into every area of your life. If you ever feel yourself getting overwhelmed, come back to this book and remind yourself that life is a work in progress, it's never supposed to be perfect. Nothing in nature is perfect and that's what makes it so beautiful and profound.

Calm your senses

A beautiful playlist and prompts to calm your mind
and get your ready for your new journey inwards

I find music to be a really great tool to use to create a nice atmosphere and headspace. The power of music is magical. I've chosen a list of songs that guided me along as I sat and wrote every word of this book. I felt it important to share as this music crafted the mindset and headspace I was in whilst these words poured out of me.

They go hand in hand. Music isn't always about the lyrics but the feeling the music gives you. I hope these songs fill your soul and make you feel whole, calm and grounded.

An Intentional Life Spotify Playlist [6]

For Now - Kina Grannis
La Vie En Rose - Emily Watts
Brave - Riley Pearce
From Gold - Novo Amor
Adrift - Hollow Coves
Spirit Cold - Tall Heights
Coffee - Beabadoobee
Dream A Little Dream -Kina Grannis
Tomorrow - Jake Issac, The Kingdom Choir
Stay With me - Angus & Julia Stone
Broken Feather - Harrison Storm
Be Yourself - Harrison Storm
Shiver - Lucy Rose
Cartoon People - Billie Marten
Re:Stacks - Bon Iver
Wild Roads - Elle Grace
Bad Apple - Billie Marten
She - Doodie
The Whisp Sings - Winter Aid
Blessings - Hollow Coves
I Do Adore - Mindy Gledhill
Would You Be So Kind - Doodie
Don't You Worry - Oh Wonder

This book has been beautiful to write, a collection of everything I have learned during my time on this earth so far. As I sit here writing this final chapter snuggled up in my big old marshmallow of a bed, I have the most delightful fluffy socks on and feel truly content. The window is cracked just slightly and I can hear the low chatter of geese and chickens from the farm close by. I can also occasionally hear a gentle murmur as people walk past the windows on their afternoon walk, all bundled up protected from the cold late-autumnal day.

The sky is grey and the atmosphere feels heavy, like we're due some rainfall, oh how perfect that would be. Echo and Rory, my two beautiful cats and companions are snuggled up together at the foot of the bed looking as cosy and content as ever. I can hear the gentle whir of the central heating which is busy warming my little cottage, oh how truly grateful I am.

I feel a warmth in my heart and a wave of gratitude for you, the reader, taking the time to read my words. Thank you for being here and for being open to receiving my message. I'm honored to be able to share my thoughts and experience with you and know that my words will be able to help you on your own journey.

My hope is that you can use this book to find deeper purpose in your own life. A calmer, more content and intentional life. A life filled with joy, passion, creativity and a sense of time that you've never felt before. I hope you never take your life for granted and that you set yourself meaningful goals and push yourself to meet them. I hope you take time to enjoy the simple things in life a whole lot more and remember to stop and look around from time to time.

Always remember to look up when you're out in nature and remember what it feels like to feel small with big trees cascading above you swaying in the wind.

Remember you're a part of something much bigger than you; allow yourself to be humbled more often. I hope you start to feel the sun on your skin on warmer days and the way it makes your hair follicles tingle and on cooler days, the soft brush of clothing on your body with the delicate scent of fabric softener lingering in the air. I want you to get comfortable with embracing change and really start to treat yourself with the kindness and love that you know that you deserve.

A life that is loved

is a life well lived

Although this book has now come to an end you can always get that calm feeling back by using the tools and guidance I have shared with you. Don't let this book be another beautiful item that collects dust on a shelf.

Write in it, highlight it, turn corners over, read it in the bath, on the beach, put your mug on it and let it be part of your home… Re-read it. Use it. Love it for its perfect imperfections.

Pop on the Intentional Living playlist, open the windows, do some goal setting, light a candle, put on your favourite comfy clothes and set about doing something you love. Dance, write, play, draw, knit, cook, bake, clean, declutter, rest. Never forget, the power is in your hands to transform and turn your life around. Day by day. Slowly but surely. Each day you live life with more intention is another day well lived.

Take care my dear friend.
This is your journey, make it a beautiful one.

Kay x

References

1. https://www.mayoclinic.org/healthylifestyle/stres
   s-management/in-depth/stress/art-
   2004603
2. https://go.roberts.edu/leadingedge/the-
   greatchoices-of-strategic-leaders
3. https://www.psychologytoday.com/gb/blog/stretc
   hing-theory/201809/how-many-decisions-do-
   wemake-each-day
4. https://www.healthline.com/health/how-
   longdoes-it-take-to-form-a-habit#takeaway
5. https://www.merriamwebster.com/dictionary/hab
   it
6. https://open.spotify.com/playlist/4L9f0vwhEc7V
   FWrD2t6HDQ?si=7248854bec9e446b
   (kayanddom: Intentional)

Acknowledgements

A special thank you to my family and friends for your amazing support and encouragement along the way especially my Mum & Nannan who have cheered me on since the day I was born. Always there to give me a hug when I need one and to keep me moving towards my dreams.

A huge thank you to my fiancé Dom & my future mother-in-law Diane for taking great care, time and patience to edit this book. I appreciate you both so much and this book literally wouldn't exist without your help and advice!

Josey my wonderful best friend, kindred spirit and the most talented photographer I know, the images you took for this book are absolutely stunning. Thank you for always checking in with me, making me laugh when you know I need to relax a little and for keeping me motivated.

And to my wonderful community of like-minded souls who have supported my vision from the day I put it out into the universe. Your support, kindness, generosity and love never goes unnoticed, I'm grateful every single day. Thank you.

This book has been a lifetime in the making for me. I've always had a big dream of writing my own book one day and now look, it's here! Wow.

Without all of your incredible support I wouldn't be where I am right now, so thank you all **so** much.

All my love,
Kay x

If you'd like to hear more from me or for further reading, videos, mindset coaching, slow living content or to join my amazing community of like-minded souls, please visit my website:

www.livingthelifeyoulove.co.uk
www.youtube.com/c/Livingthelifeyoulove

living the life you love

live simply ~ simply live

Printed in Great Britain
by Amazon